ROTATION
PLAN

THE THEATRE
OF OPERATIONS
1796-1797

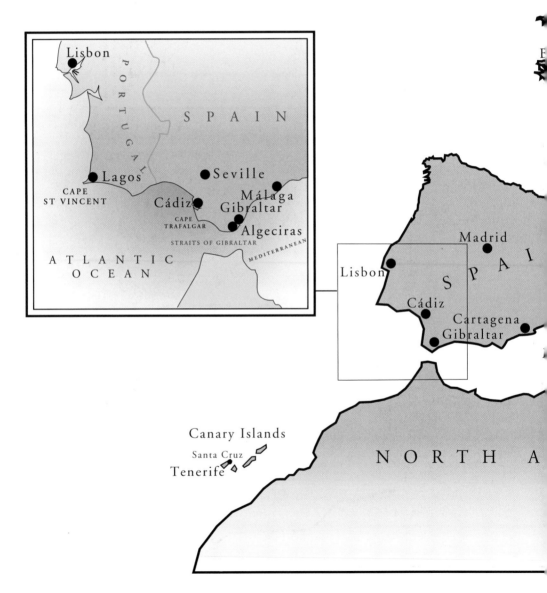

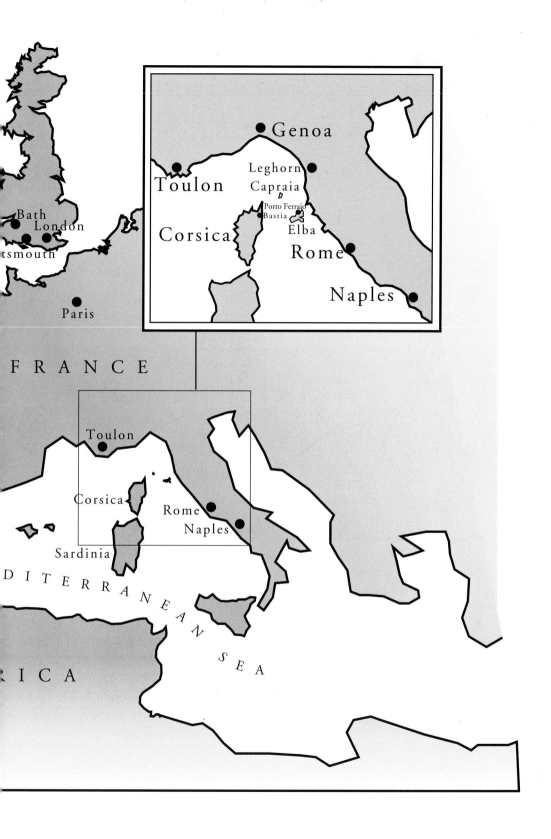

Genoa

Toulon

Leghorn

Capraia

Corsica

Porto Ferraio
Bastia

Elba

Rome

Naples

Bath
London

tsmouth

Paris

FRANCE

Toulon

Corsica

Rome

Naples

Sardinia

MEDITERRANEAN

SEA

RICA

1797

NELSON'S
YEAR *of*
DESTINY

Also by Colin White

The End of the Sailing Navy
The Heyday of Steam
The Nelson Companion
The Nelson Encyclopaedia
Nelson – The New Letters
The Trafalgar Captains – their lives and memorials
Nelson the Admiral

1797

NELSON'S
YEAR *of*
DESTINY

Cape St Vincent and
Santa Cruz de Tenerife

COLIN WHITE

SUTTON PUBLISHING LIMITED

To My Dear Nieces

Jennifer White
Elizabeth White
Sarah White

First published in the United Kingdom in 1998 by
Sutton Publishing Ltd · Phoenix Mill · Thrupp · Stroud · Gloucestershire
In association with the Royal Naval Museum

Paperback edition first published in 2001
Second paperback edition published in 2006

British Library Cataloguing in Publication Data
A catalogue record for this book is available from the British Library

ISBN 0 7509 3752 1

Typeset in 10/13 Sabon.
Typesetting and origination by
Sutton Publishing Limited.
Printed in Great Britain by
J.H. Haynes & Co Ltd, Sparkford.

Contents

PART THREE
The attack on Santa Cruz de Tenerife, July 1797

List of Illustrations

SOURCES

RNM:	Royal Naval Museum
NMM:	National Maritime Museum
MMRC:	Museo Militar Regional de Canarias
SNR:	Society for Nautical Research
Monmouth:	Nelson Museum, Monmouth

PLANS

Endpapers: The Theatre of Operations in the Western Mediterranean and Atlantic

Acknowledgements

I am most fortunate to be working at the Royal Naval Museum at a particularly exciting time in its history. Not only is the Museum itself expanding rapidly, with new exhibitions and initiatives constantly under way, but it has also, in conjunction with HMS *Victory*, become the focal point for many of the events associated with the Nelson Decade. As a result, it is a melting pot for the new insights that are emerging about Nelson and his times and a key player in the drive to make those insights available to a wider audience.

My first thanks, therefore, go to my Museum colleagues who have encouraged me to write this book and who have helped me in its production. Chief among them is the Director, Campbell McMurray, under whose wise leadership the Museum's reputation for scholarship and professional excellence has been so greatly enhanced. He has given me generous support, including allowing me the luxury of time off to write the text in comparative peace when there were so many other calls on our energies. I am also grateful to Chris Howard Bailey, the Museum's Director of Publications, whose shrewd advice on the structure of the book has been decisive and her experience of publishing so reassuring; to my colleagues in the Curatorial Department, Matthew Sheldon, Deborah Potter and Allison Wareham, who so cheerfully made time to help me select illustrations from our rich and largely untapped collections when they were already fully stretched with other work; to my PA, Helen Gooding, who has dealt so efficiently with all the additional administrative tasks; to Michael O'Callaghan of CDA Design, who prepared all the maps and plans, to Michael Forder, who prepared the index and to Chris Arkell and Denise Smith of our Trading Company, who have handled all the business and financial aspects of the project. At Sutton Publishing, I would like to thank my editors Jonathan Falconer and Alison Flowers and the designer Martin Latham.

I also owe a large debt to my Spanish colleagues, chief among them my good friend Agustín Guimerá Ravina of the Centro de Estudios Historicos in Madrid. He shared the results of his own researches with me without reserve, arranged for me to visit Tenerife to attend a key conference, at which most of the new insights from the Spanish sources were unveiled, and also took me on a memorable walking tour of the battle site itself. I am also grateful to his colleague in Madrid, Hugo O'Donnell and, in Tenerife, to Coronel Juan Tous Meliá of the Museo Militar Regional de Canarias and José Garcia Perez of the Universida de la Laguna – all of whom have helped me with research and with finding suitable illustrations.

My third key debt is to that splendid band of Nelson enthusiasts, The 1805 Club – and in particular to their current Chairman, Stephen Howarth, and his predecessor, Michael Nash. It was the Club's invitation, two years ago, to write a monograph on the Battle of Cape St Vincent which first engaged my interest and their generous patronage which enabled the results of my researches to first see the light of day. They have very kindly allowed me to recycle the material (originally published by the Club in February 1997) to form part of this book. Thanks too, for support and encouragement, to my fellow members of the 'St Vincent 200' Conference Committee: Peter Warwick, Peter Goodwin, Louis Hodgkin and Brian Lavery.

The book draws heavily on the work and goodwill of many other friends and colleagues, all of whom have been extraordinarily generous with their help and advice. Anne-Marie Hills and Leslie LeQuesne have helped me with the sections on Nelson's wounds and Richard Walker with information about the portraits; John Curtis, Curator of the Lloyd's Nelson Collection, allowed me access to their fascinating collection of Nelson letters and gave me permission to publish the hitherto unknown description of the Battle of Cape St Vincent by Ralph Miller which I discovered among them (see Appendix One); Kirstie Buckland allowed me a preview of Miller's account of Cádiz and Tenerife which she recently discovered among the Molyneaux papers; Christopher Gray of the National Maritime Museum helped in locating illustrations from their wonderful collection of drawings and prints; Andrew Helme of the Nelson Museum in Monmouth gave permission to reproduce the splendid watercolour drawing of Nelson from his collection (see p. 113) and David Price, Organist and Master of the Choristers at Portsmouth Cathedral, helped me to reconstruct the music played at the Grand Thanksgiving Service in St Paul's on 19 December 1797.

Because of this remarkable level of support and encouragement – so generously and warmly given in every case – my path has been considerably eased and, as a result, writing this book has been a most enjoyable task. But, as always, the demands its creation have made upon my time and energy have forced me to be very anti-social. So my last, and warmest, thanks go to my family and friends who have sustained me throughout the process and, above all, to my dear, and long-suffering, Peter.

Colin White
Royal Naval Museum, 10 April 1998

Preface to the Second Edition

From trail-blazer to standard work

1797: Nelson's Year of Destiny was deliberately conceived as a trail-blazer. In my original introduction (see pp. xiii–xiv) I explained how the book had arisen out of all the new information that had emerged as a result of the bicentenary conferences, and other research projects in 1997. I suggested that the new material demonstrated that there was an urgent need for a thorough re-evaluation of the existing Nelson primary source material. I also highlighted the need for a full-scale bicentenary biography, based on extensive and completely new research, rather than being another re-hash of the familiar material. I tried to show, by looking at one year – 1797 – just how dramatically the old story could be refreshed and revitalised.

As 2005 comes to a close, I think it is fair to say that this book achieved its aims. Since 1998, there has been a flood of new research material. Over 1,000 unpublished Nelson letters have been located; each of Nelson's battles has been thoroughly re-evaluated, with the help of historians from the former 'opposition'; studies of the late eighteenth century Royal Navy, and of other key figures in it, have placed Nelson more squarely in his context. And this new material has led to the creation of an armada of new biographies and battle-studies, almost all of them featuring at least some of the new material – at the last count, more than 35 new titles in 2005 alone.

My own main contribution to the 2005 fleet has been two new books. *Nelson: The New Letters* (Boydell and Brewer) features 500 of the most important of the new letters located by the 'Nelson Letters Project', set up by the Royal Naval Museum, in the wake of the discoveries of 1997, to revisit and analyse the Nelsonian primary source material. *Nelson the Admiral* (Sutton) takes a fresh look at Nelson as a professional sea-commander, using this new material. Because *1797* has been so successful, I decided not to recycle its material for the new book but, instead, to start *Admiral* where *1797* ends – with the great Naval Thanksgiving Service in St Paul's Cathedral. So *1797* and *Nelson the Admiral* are companion volumes and need to be read together to get the full picture of Nelson's development as a commander. I am therefore most grateful to Sutton Publishing for inviting me to prepare this new, second edition of *1797* to sit alongside its sequel.

A number of small changes have been made to the text, to bring the book in line with current research, but I have been pleasantly surprised by how well the main arguments and judgements have stood the test of time and ongoing debate. Moreover, every account of Nelson's 1797 exploits published since 1998 has been based on my narrative and has quoted my conclusions – even the battle-plans have been copied, rather than new ones prepared! It seems, then, that the 'trail-blazer' has matured into the standard work.

The Anchorage, Portsmouth
200th anniversary of Nelson's State Funeral

Introduction

In May 1810, Captain James Bowen RN, then a Commissioner of the Transport Board, received a package from Tenerife. Inside, he found the gold seals, watch chain and sword that had once belonged to his brother, Captain Richard Bowen, who had been killed during the abortive British attack on Santa Cruz de Tenerife in July 1797. With the relics was a letter explaining that they had formerly been displayed in the Town House at Santa Cruz but that, as Spain and Britain were now allies, the town officials 'did not wish to retain a trophy which could remind them that they had ever been opposed to each other'.

Anyone who was involved in the impressive and moving commemorations of the bicentenaries of the Battle of Cape St Vincent in Portsmouth in February 1997, and the attack on Santa Cruz in Tenerife the following July, will recognize that sentiment. Both events were conducted in a heart-warming spirit of reconciliation and international friendship and there was, above all, a rich sharing of scholarly insights. As a result, British historians were able to appreciate more fully the difficulties under which the Spanish fleet was labouring at Cape St Vincent and to learn about the effects on the Spanish economy of the British blockade of Cádiz. They also discovered that Nelson was opposed at Tenerife, not by 8,000 regular troops, as has always been supposed, but by a force of only 1,669, more than half of whom were hastily summoned militiamen, armed only with sickles. This book draws extensively on all this new Spanish material and so presents, really for the first time, a truly balanced narrative of both operations.

Such sharing of information, and broadening of scholarly horizons, is directly in line with the aims of the 'Nelson Decade'. When the Royal Naval Museum and the National Maritime Museum jointly launched the Decade in October 1995 it was always their intention to ensure that it did not become simply an excuse for chauvinistic jollification. Their hope was that the glamour of Nelson's name could be used to encourage research into the less familiar aspects of the period and thus draw attention to the richness of Britain's maritime heritage. The results of 1997 events have so far been very encouraging. They include a new study of the life and career of Sir John Jervis; new insights into the British tactics at the Battle of Cape

St Vincent and the discovery of fascinating new primary source material relating to the battle, the blockade of Cádiz and the attack on Santa Cruz. Again, all this material has been used in the preparation of this book and so it has been possible to set Nelson's exploits in their wider operational and political context.

As its contribution to the Nelson Decade, the Royal Naval Museum has launched its own Nelson Bicentenary Project. At its heart is a new and mould-breaking exhibition, 'Horatio Nelson: the Hero and the Man', which will offer many new insights based on careful research and scholarship. This is supported by an ambitious publishing initiative through which the Museum will seek to explore many different aspects of modern Nelson studies. Our hope is that this project will culminate in the publication of a large-scale biography which will draw together all the new insights and research material into a single new narrative. As part of the preliminary research for such a work, I have begun a gradual revisitation of all the available Nelson primary source material – a process which has already shown that the great printed sources, upon which we have relied for so long, are now incomplete and even at times inaccurate. We urgently need a new and definitive edition of Nelson's correspondence, drawn directly from the original material.

In the meantime, however, the available material needs to be subjected to searching textual analysis and this is the method I have employed in preparing this book. Where do some of the long-established stories and judgements about Nelson originate? Is the original source reliable? When we ask questions like this some interesting changes to the familiar story occur. On the one hand, we can bid farewell to the melodramatic shout Nelson is supposed to have uttered as he boarded the *San José* at Cape St Vincent, 'Westminster Abbey or glorious victory!' – it was almost certainly an invention of Emma Hamilton's. On the other hand, we can also discard the suggestion that he ordered the disastrous second attack at Tenerife simply because he was overconfident and contemptuous of the Spanish. A recently discovered account of Tenerife by Captain Ralph Miller (to be published by The 1805 Club) allows us to eavesdrop, for the first time, on the council of war at which the proposal to renew the attack was discussed and, as a result, a very different picture emerges.

This book, then, has two main purposes. First, it seeks to draw together all the new material that has emerged about the events of 1797 and to blend it with re-evaluated existing material, thus creating a new narrative of one of the most critical years in Nelson's life. In that sense it is a synthesis: looking back over the last eighteen months and summing up the insights that have been gained. Second, it looks forward to the planned bicentenary biography and offers a model for how such a project might be approached. In that sense, it is 'work in progress' and both I, and my colleagues at the Royal Naval Museum, will be very grateful for comments and contributions from anyone who reads this book and who shares our desire to bring Nelson alive for a new generation and a new century.

A Note About the
Layout

This book is a combination of new material that has emerged as a result of recent research and a re-evaluation of the 'old' material. Naturally, where my conclusions challenge the accepted story, readers will wish to know what evidence I can muster to support my case. However, the problem with digressions of this sort is that they interrupt the flow of the narrative and my overriding aim has been to tell a good story – albeit one based on meticulous research.

Of course, the usual way of dealing with this sort of explanatory material is to banish it to notes and, as a result, some of the most interesting insights in the book are often hidden away. I have always felt this is a waste and, in any case, the new insights are the chief *raison d'être* of this particular work. So, with the help of colleagues at the Museum and at Sutton Publishing, I have decided to try an experimental structure. Most of the speculative material has been placed in special boxes, together with supporting references for my conclusions, thus leaving the main narrative free of lengthy diversions. Additionally, detailed comments about my sources – especially where these are new, or not generally known – appear at the end of each part. Lastly, there is a full Bibliography at the end of the book.

Porto Ferraio, Elba: scene of General de Burgh's Christmas Ball. Captain Fremantle's frigate, HMS Inconstant, lies at anchor, left foreground.

PROLOGUE

The Theatre, Port Ferraio, Elba,

25 December 1796

On Christmas Day, 1796, Lieutenant General John de Burgh, the commanding officer of the British forces in Elba, gave a ball. The island's only town, Porto Ferraio, picturesquely clustered on the sides of a commanding hill at the mouth of the bay and crammed inside its defending walls, was small and the only building large enough for such an event was the theatre. So it was commandeered by the British troops, who cleared out the seats and installed special decorations.

The day was overcast and, shortly before the ball began, there was a sudden flurry of rain; this did not deter the 300 guests, who packed themselves cheerfully into the improvised ballroom. It was, of course, a predominantly military occasion, so there was much service gossip and some heavy drinking: Captain Woodhouse of the Royal Navy, recently appointed Port Captain, disgraced himself by getting drunk in celebration. But there were also civilians present, including ladies from Corsica and Italy and two from England, 'in the shape of Pyramids'.

That tart observation comes from the diary of seventeen-year-old Eugenia Wynne, an English girl who was present with her father, Robert Wynne, her mother, Agathe, and her four sisters. They had recently taken refuge in British-occupied Elba after their leisurely tour of Europe had been brusquely interrupted by the sudden invasion of the northern Italian states by a French army under General Napoleon Bonaparte. Evacuated from Leghorn by the frigate HMS *Inconstant* under Captain Thomas Fremantle, they spent four months as the guests of the Mediterranean Fleet, where the attractive and talented Wynne sisters soon became the favourites of the officers – who christened them 'The Amiables'.

Elizabeth Wynne (known to all as 'Betsey') fell in love with their rescuer, Thomas Fremantle and, even though her father disapproved of a match with an impecunious naval officer, Fremantle kept in touch with the family. On the evening of the ball he sent his barge to convey them to the town, where they changed into their ballgowns at the house of some Italian friends, the Cantinis.

As the guests gathered, one topic of conversation predominated. Commodore Horatio Nelson, who five months earlier had masterminded the occupation of Elba, had arrived that morning in HMS *La Minerve* and the rumour was circulating that he had come to take command of the island. On his way from Gibraltar, Nelson had fallen in with a large Spanish frigate and, after a fierce action, had captured her. Unfortunately, the arrival of a Spanish squadron had forced him to give up his prize but, nonetheless, the fiery commodore had added further to his already considerable reputation for dash and bravery. It was only a small victory but, at a time when the war was going very badly for Britain and her allies, it was a welcome shaft of light.

So it was that when Nelson arrived at the ball, accompanied by Captains Cockburn and Fremantle, he was given a hero's welcome. General de Burgh himself greeted him formally at the door and as he entered the ballroom the band struck up 'See the conquering hero comes' and then played 'Rule Britannia' as an encore.

The ball was a great success. Eugenia and her sisters 'danced a great deal and amused ourselves very much' and spent the rest of the time surveying the very assorted company, whom they quickly dubbed 'ridiculous'. Having changed back into their travelling clothes at the house of the obliging Cantinis, the Wynnes finally returned home in Fremantle's barge at about four in the morning, very tired but happy.

Nelson, too, was happy and wrote proudly to his elder brother William to tell him of his flattering reception at the ball – although, with becoming modesty he said only that 'one particular tune was played' and did not actually name it. Although within the Royal Navy itself he was recognized as a rising star, public recognition for his services had so far eluded him. Now, he had been hailed as a hero – and he found that he liked the experience: 'I am loaded with compliments,' he told his brother and then added more thoughtfully, 'it is true these are given on the spot, what England may think I know not.'

Less than six weeks later he would give England plenty to think about. His year of destiny had begun.

PART ONE

Nelson in the Mediterranean, September 1796–January 1797

Miniature of Captain Horatio Nelson painted in Leghorn in 1794. He is wearing the undress uniform of a captain. This was Fanny Nelson's favourite picture of her husband, which she kept in a special casket.

CHAPTER ONE

'Our Gallant Commodore'
Nelson in 1796

*'When I reflect that I have had the unbounded confidence of three
Commanders-in-chief I cannot but feel a conscious pride.'*
Nelson to his wife, 24 April 1796

COMMODORE HORATIO NELSON

The man who strode confidently into the improvised ballroom in Porto Ferraio looked very different to the Nelson we know from his portraits, most of which were painted after wounds and suffering had prematurely aged him. At thirty-eight he was still in his vigorous prime: a miniature painted in Leghorn in 1794 (opposite), shows a slim, handsome and almost boyish man with large intense eyes and an unruly mop of sandy-grey hair. Nelson's stepson Josiah Nisbet did not think it a good likeness, but most of Nelson's friends disagreed and his wife, Fanny Nelson, always treasured it, even after she had more up-to-date portraits in her possession. Perhaps it reminded her of happier days, before the break-up of their marriage: certainly, it has an innocence about it that the later, more self-confident and heroic portraits lack.

At that time, Nelson was in excellent health. After enduring the sweltering summers of the West Indies and the freezing winters of Norfolk, he had at last found in the Mediterranean a climate that suited his constitution. 'I fancy you will find me grown very stout,' he had told Fanny, at the beginning of the year, 'and my health was never better than at this moment.'

He had, of course, been blinded in his right eye when he was struck in the face by a shower of gravel while directing the naval guns at the siege of Calvi in Corsica in 1794. But, now that the superficial wounds had healed, the loss was not apparent and no one appears to have noticed it. Indeed, he himself never referred to his 'blind' eye at this time: it would seem that he had soon learned to live with his disability.

Nelson's height

The popular myth that Nelson was an unusually small man has proved remarkably persistent – despite conclusive evidence to the contrary. He was in fact between 5 ft 6 in and 5 ft 7 in tall (c. 1.7 m) – in other words around the average height for man of his time. This conclusion is based chiefly on a detailed study of his 'Trafalgar' uniform coat, waistcoat and breeches carried out by Lesley Edwards of 'Stitch in Time' in preparation for the creation of an exact copy commissioned by the Royal Naval Museum. Her study also established that Nelson had a chest measurement of about 38/39 in (96/99 cm) and a waist size of about 32/33 in (81/83 cm).

The conclusion about his height is supported by contemporary descriptions. For example, an American, Benjamin Silliman, who saw him in September 1805 said he was 'of about middle height, or rather more'. (Pocock, p. 309)

Nor do any of the contemporary references to him make mention of his stature and physique – from which it seems fair to assume that they were unremarkable. It was his energy that people remembered most vividly; his boyish eagerness and almost naïve frankness; what Lady Minto (who first met him in Corsica at this time when her husband, Sir Gilbert Elliot, was appointed Viceroy) later called, his 'honest, simple manners'.

In Nelson's case, good health and personal happiness were usually linked to professional success. He had a tendency to psychosomatic illness and so was usually at his lowest ebb when his career was not going well for some reason, 'If I ever feel unwell, it is when I have no active employment, that is but seldom,' he told Fanny.

When he wrote these words in August 1796, he was generally happy with the progress of his career. Having served in the Mediterranean since the beginning of the war, he had taken part in most of the key operations, including two indecisive fleet actions with the French, as well as the capture of Corsica and of Elba. Now, he was a commodore in command of a detached squadron off the north-west coast of Italy, watching the advance of the victorious French armies under General Bonaparte and doing all that he could to hamper them. He had a fine new ship, HMS *Captain*, with a well-trained ship's company, including a large contingent who had already served with him for three years in his former command, HMS *Agamemnon*. Most important, he had an excellent corps of officers, including a number of his own protégés, or 'followers' – lads such as Midshipman William

Hoste and Lieutenant John Weatherhead, both, like him, the sons of Norfolk parsons – and headed by a man he had picked himself, thirty-year-old Captain Ralph Miller, widely recognized as one of the rising stars in the fleet.

He also had the ear, and the confidence, of his commander-in-chief. At this time, the rank of commodore, with the right to fly a distinguishing swallow-tailed flag, or 'pendant', was a temporary appointment, often in the personal gift of the local senior officer. So Nelson's detached command was a clear sign that he was well-regarded by Admiral Sir John Jervis, who had taken command of the Mediterranean Fleet in December 1795.

NELSON IN ACTION – SEPTEMBER 1796

The qualities which had earned Nelson the trust of his admiral were well demonstrated in the space of just one month in the autumn of 1796. (For a map illustrating his operations, see the endpapers.) At the beginning of September, he was off the port of Leghorn (Livorno) in HMS *Captain*, where his squadron was

The French capture Livorno (Leghorn) 30 June 1796. As the French troops march along the dockside, the British ships, packed with refugees, get under way (top right). A few weeks later, Nelson arrived with his squadron to enforce a strict blockade of the port.

Genoa Roads, c. 1830. It was here, on 11 September 1796, that HMS Captain *was fired on by the Genoese batteries, thus provoking Nelson's attack on the island of Capraia.*

blockading the port, following the occupation of the town by a detachment of General Bonaparte's invading French army. Nelson enforced the blockade strictly but with a touch of humanity – as, for example, when he compelled a Danish merchant vessel to return to port instead of seizing her as, by law, he was entitled to do. But his ultimate aim was clear; as he wrote to his old friend Captain Cuthbert Collingwood, then serving in Jervis' fleet in command of the battleship, HMS *Excellent*, 'Sometimes I hope, and then despair of getting these starved Leghornese to cut the throats of this French crew', adding with characteristic irony, 'What an idea for a Christian! I hope there is a great latitude for us in the next world.'

At the same time as he was organising the blockade, Nelson was also gathering military and political intelligence, which he passed to Jervis. Two of his informants were women: one, an opera singer Adelaide Correglia, had been his mistress some years before in Leghorn. The other, Frances Caffarena the wife of a merchant in Genoa, gave him valuable information – including advance news of the Spanish entry into war.

From Leghorn, Nelson sailed on 3 September to Genoa. Although the city was supposedly neutral, pressure from the French had forced the Genoese to close their ports against British ships. A drove of cattle was waiting there to be transported to

Nelson and Adelaide Correglia

The gradual emergence of our understanding of Signorina Correglia's small but telling role in Nelson's story shows how modern research is still piecing together some of the minutiae of Nelson's life from a number of different sources.

The existence of his Leghornese mistress went unnoticed until 1958, when Oliver Warner first mentioned her in his biography, *A Portrait of Lord Nelson* (pp. 91–3). He quoted extracts from the diary of Captain Thomas Fremantle, which make it clear that Fremantle rather disapproved of her, writing for example: 'August 1795. Dined with Nelson. Dolly aboard who has a sort of abscess in her side. He makes himself ridiculous with that woman.' In referring to a 'dolly' Fremantle was using the slang word for a mistress, rather than the woman's name and, in fact, her identity was not known until the 1970s, when a letter from Nelson in schoolboy French was discovered in the Henry E. Huntingdon Library at San Martino California:

Ma Chere Adelaide Je Suis partant en cette moment pour la Mere, une Vaisseau Neopolitan partir avec moi pour Livorne, Croire Moi toujours Votre Chere Amie Horatio Nelson. Avez Vous bien Successe (Huntington Library: HM 34180)

The final piece in the jigsaw was discovered as recently as 1989, when some documents were sold at Christie's which showed that, even after the French occupation, Nelson continued to send Adelaide money through an English merchant.

It would appear that Nelson's liaison with Adelaide was fairly well-known among his colleagues - and even with his commander-in-chief, Sir John Jervis, who wrote to him sending 'compliments to la belle Adelaide'. This lack of shame or concealment about his relationship with her is an interesting precursor of his later very public affirmation of his love for Emma Hamilton.

The Capraia ultimatum

The ultimatum which Nelson issued to the Genoese authorities in Capraia is of particular interest because it appears to have formed the basis of the more famous one he later prepared for use at Tenerife in July 1797.

The Capraia ultimatum, dated 18 September 1796, is printed on pages 273–4 in volume II of Nicolas. The wording was drawn from the written instructions Nelson had received from Elliot (also printed by Nicolas) which laid strong emphasis on the need to deal sensitively with the local population. Key phrases include: 'All people in the Civil Department to be continued in the Offices which they at present hold', 'All inhabitants of the Town and Island are assured of perfect security for their persons, property and religion . . . the present laws will be preserved', 'No contribution will be demanded'.

Almost identical phrases occur in the Tenerife ultimatum, which reinforces the view that Nelson based his plans for the capture of Santa Cruz on his earlier, successful operation at Capraia (see note on p. 106).

the British fleet – a vital source of fresh meat at a time when supplies were increasingly difficult to obtain. Arriving off the port and finding that the British minister was absent, Nelson sent a polite, formal note to the Doge, expressing a hope that 'there is some mistake in the matter'. But the French were there before him and had set up their batteries. After a few days of tense stand-off, the *Captain* was fired on and the commodore was brusquely informed that all the ports of the Republic were now closed to British ships.

Nelson immediately cast about for the most effective way to make the Genoese aware of the power of the British fleet. Just to the north-east of Corsica lay the small Genoese-held island of Capraia: a thorn in the side of the British, since it acted as a safe haven for French privateers. Nelson now decided to seize the island and so he hurried to Bastia to consult with the British Viceroy of Corsica, Sir Gilbert Elliot (for a note about Elliot see p. 19). Arriving on 14 September, he had no difficulty in persuading Elliot to support him and, less than twenty-four hours later, he was at sea again with two transports carrying troops of the 69th Regiment and 51st Foot, under the command of Major John Logan.

A textbook combined operation followed: 'I do not believe the two services ever more cordially united than on the present occasion,' Nelson later reported to Elliot. The troops were landed at the north end of the island, while seamen manhandled a battery of cannon up a mountain commanding the main town, 'with their usual spirit and alacrity,' as Nelson later told Jervis. As soon as their forces were in position, Nelson and Logan sent in an ultimatum, demanding the surrender of the island, 'to the Arms of His Britannic Majesty' in order to prevent, 'an effusion of blood and all the other consequences of a refusal'. Faced with such a powerful and well-positioned force, the Genoese 'Padri del Commune' duly capitulated and so Capraia fell into the hands of the British on 19 September without any bloodshed on either side, barely a week after the *Captain* had been fired upon in Genoa Roads. Retribution had been swift and ruthlessly efficient.

So, Nelson could show great rigour in pursuit of his aims, although always tinged with humanity, as seen in his blockade of Leghorn. He could be single-mindedly direct, as when dealing with the complex diplomatic machinations in Genoa itself and he could act speedily, as in his lightning attack on Capraia. This combination of qualities marked him out as unusual.

It is also interesting to note – especially in the light of what was to follow in 1797 – that the Capraia operation was conducted without any consultation with Jervis. Speed was essential if the attack was to have maximum impact on the Genoese and so, with Elliot's support, Nelson was prepared to make the decision to attack himself, without wasting time trying to contact his admiral. Earlier, in February, he had told Fanny that Jervis, 'seems at present to consider me as an assistant more than a subordinate for I am acting without orders', and his actions at Capraia show that he trusted Jervis to support him when he acted on his own initiative. That trust was amply rewarded for, when he fowarded a copy of Nelson's official report on the Capraia operation to the Admiralty, Jervis commented that it 'reflects the highest honour on his skill, judgment and enterprize'.

Nelson was proud of Jervis' approval and with reason, for it was never given lightly. His letters home, especially to his wife, show that he was well aware that his admiral's good reports were having an important effect. The influential First Lord of the Admiralty, Lord Spencer, was beginning to take notice of him and so within the Royal Navy itself his reputation was already well established. But the same letters also betray a strong longing, even a craving, for more. As his father, the Revd Edmund Nelson put it, writing in his idiosyncratic style to his youngest daughter Kitty Matcham in December 1796, 'If He can live by compliments from the Great and Powerfull, no want, but We Hope they are a prelude to more Substantials.'

Chief among the 'substantials' for which Nelson longed was popular acclaim. A constant theme in his private letters to Fanny and the rest of his family throughout 1796 was the lack of public recognition for his deeds. At that time, the main way in which an officer's achievements became known at home was through the official dispatches published in the *London Gazette*. Nelson had hoped for this sort of accolade when he had played such a key role in the capture of Corsica in 1794; but he had been disappointed to find that his name appeared hardly at all in any of the public accounts. Since then his exploits had been important and arduous, but unglamorous, and he was aware that none of them would win him the fame he so coveted. In a letter to Fanny, dated 2 August when he was wearing himself out in the blockade of Leghorn, he gave vent to his frustration:

> . . . had all my actions been gazetted not one fortnight would have passed. Let those enjoy their brag and one day or other I will have a large Gazette to myself. I feel that one day or other such an opportunity will be given me. I cannot if I am in the field of glory be kept out of sight. . . . Probably my services will be forgot (by the Great) by the time I get home but my own mind will not

---

Nelson's letters to his wife

The version of Nelson's famous 'gazette' letter to Fanny quoted here, differs in some important respects from the version printed in Nicolas (vol. II, pp. 230–1). In fact, nearly all Fanny's letters in Nicolas have been badly mangled and should be regarded with suspicion.

To be fair, Nicolas was well aware of this problem: he was unable to gain access to Nelson's letters to Fanny and so had to rely on the extracts published in the earlier, semi-official biography by the Revd James Stanier Clarke and John M'Arthur published in 1809. Nicolas always suspected that Clarke and M'Arthur had 'improved' the letters and we now know that he was right, thanks to the unexpurgated versions published by George Naish in his meticulous work of scholarship, *Nelson's letters to his wife*.

In Clarke's turgid transcripts, with all the risqué remarks and irrelevancies omitted, the grammar corrected, and with extensive, plodding punctuation, Nelson often sounds as stilted and portentous as Clarke himself. In the original letters on the other hand Nelson's thoughts tumble out of him in an exhilarating stream of consciousness jumping from idea to idea with minimal punctuation in a way that gives us a tantalising echo of what his conversation must have sounded like. It is these versions which have been used throughout this book.

forget nor fail to feel a degree of consolation and applause superior to undeserved rewards. Wherever there is anything to do, there providence is sure to direct my steps, and ever credit must be given to me in spite of envy.

However, even as Nelson wrote his complaint to Fanny, his chance for glory was drawing near. Elsewhere in Europe, events were combining to bring about a major change in British fortunes in the Mediterranean and, once again, he was to play a leading role in the events that were unfolding.

The town and fortifications of Bastia, Corsica: evacuated by Nelson in October 1796.

CHAPTER TWO

'A measure which I cannot approve'
The British evacuate the Mediterranean

'One day or other I will have a large Gazette to myself.'
Nelson to his wife, 2 August 1796

THE COLLAPSE OF THE FIRST COALITION

At the outset of war, in 1793, Prime Minister William Pitt had assembled an impressive coalition of European nations to meet the threat of French expansion but, gradually, each of the key allies had been eliminated by the French. First to go was Prussia in April 1795, followed by Holland in May. The Spanish contributed a fleet under General Juan de Langara y Huarte to assist in the capture of Toulon in 1793 and mounted an invasion of Roussillon. But, by early 1796, the French had driven the Spanish armies back through Catalonia and were threatening an invasion of central Spain. In July the Treaty of Bailea was signed which allied Spain to France and in October, concerned about British threats to her overseas territories, Spain declared war on Britain.

Pitt had hoped to persuade the Austrians to attack the French in the Rhinelands but their attention was wholly occupied elsewhere by the brilliant campaign of the young General Napoleon Bonaparte. Sweeping into Austrian-held northern Italy in mid-April, he captured Milan a month later and went on to take Florence and Leghorn in late June – the action which forced Robert Wynne and his family to seek the protection of the Royal Navy so hurriedly. Faced with such a dangerous situation, Pitt's government decided to open peace negotiations and, in October 1796, Lord Malmesbury was sent to France to discuss terms. But the victorious

French stalled and created difficulties before finally, on 20 December, giving the envoy just twenty-four hours to leave Paris. So strong did they feel themselves that, at the end of the year, they planned a direct threat to the British Isles themselves, sending a squadron from Brest to Bantry Bay in Ireland with an army aboard, intending to join with the United Irishmen and stir up a rising. Dispersed by the weather, rather than by British naval action, this unsuccessful invasion attempt served further to emphasize Britain's isolation.

Realizing that a war with Spain was imminent, and discouraged by the news of Napoleon's successes, the Cabinet decided in August that Britain's position in the Middle Sea was no longer tenable. The combined fleets of France and Spain outnumbered the twenty-two battleships that Jervis had at his disposal and the French invasion of northern Italy had cut off his main source of supplies. With a powerful Spanish fleet stationed at Cádiz, between him and Britain, his lines of communication were threatened and so the most sensible strategic solution seemed to be to withdraw the Mediterranean Fleet to a position outside the Straits of Gibraltar, where it could more easily stay in contact with the other main British fleet off Brest. This, in turn, meant that Corsica and Elba had to be evacuated, since they could not be defended without a strong naval presence. Orders to this effect reached Jervis on 25 September.

Earlier in the summer, Jervis had sent a detachment of seven ships under Rear Admiral Man to watch Cádiz. Man rejoined the main force off Corsica in August – but so precipitately that he failed to supply his ships before sailing and so Jervis was forced to send him back to Gibraltar to replenish. Now new orders were sent after him, ordering him to return to Corsica as speedily as possible. In the absence of his second in command, and preoccupied with concentrating his force and arranging for supplies, Jervis delegated the evacuation of Corsica to his trusted commodore.

Nelson was horrified and wrote to Fanny in his most Shakespearean vein, even including a direct quote from *King John*:

> We are all preparing for an evacuation of the Mediterranean, a measure which I cannot approve. At home they know not what this fleet is capable of performing, *any and everything*. Much as I shall rejoice to see England in private view, I lament in sackcloth and ashes our present orders, so dishonourable to the dignity of England, whose fleets are equal to meet the world in arms, and of all fleets I ever saw I never saw one equal in point of officers and men to our present one, and with a Commander-in-Chief fit to lead them to glory.

THE BRITISH LEAVE CORSICA

The evacuation of Corsica almost ended in disaster. Despite all attempts to keep the British intentions secret, the presence of a growing fleet of transports gave the game away and so, by the time Elliot formally gave notice of his departure to the

---

'Equal to meet the world in arms'

The passage from *King John* that Nelson refers to in his letter to Fanny is the famous patriotic claim: 'Come the three corners of the world in arms / And we shall shock them. Naught shall make us rue / If England to itself do rest but true.'

Nelson's most famous use of a Shakespearean quotation was his description of the Nile captains as 'a band of brothers' which comes from the great 'Agincourt speech' in *Henry V*; as does another quotation which he used on a number of occasions to different correspondents, 'If it be a sin to covet honour [which he usually misquoted as 'glory'] / I am the most offending soul alive'. But these were far from being isolated examples: other Shakespearean plays from which he quoted include *Othello, Julius Caesar, Henry IV Part One, Hamlet, Two Gentlemen of Verona* and *Much Ado About Nothing* (for a full list, with references, see my article, 'Nelson and Shakespeare', *Nelson Dispatch*, July 2000).

It would seem, then, that Nelson knew the plays well and had even memorized some of the key passages.

Municipality of Bastia, the Corsicans were ready to act. Understandably anxious to win the approval of their likely future masters by a display of zeal, they appointed a Committee of Thirty to take over the government of the island and started making direct approaches to the French generals in Leghorn, inviting them to send troops. The French agreed to come and told the committee to place an embargo on all British property and to forbid any vessel to leave the mole.

Nelson arrived in Bastia in the frigate *La Minerve* on 14 October to find Elliot in a dangerous situation. All the British troops had been withdrawn to the main fort (see illustration on p. 19), leaving only a guard on the viceroy's house and the army commander, Lieutenant General John de Burgh, was in a state of despair, believing it was impossible to save any stores, cannons or provisions. Nelson thought otherwise and proceeded to take control. Although a gale was blowing, he brought all his available ships to anchor close to the molehead and then bluntly informed the committee that any attempt to prevent the embarkation would be followed by a bombardment of the town. The Corsicans backed down and the laborious loading of stores and troops began.

It was a striking demonstration of the ubiquity of seapower. On 13 October all seemed lost: and, having managed to get his wife and children away to Gibraltar in

The British capture Corsica. Lord Hood's flagship, HMS Victory *(left foreground) lies off the port of Bastia, following the capture of Corsica in 1794. The town became the headquarters of the British Viceroy, Sir Gilbert Elliot.*

a fast frigate, Elliot had resigned himself to capture and imprisonment. Then, out of the blue, Nelson arrived at dawn on the 14th, coming to the house almost clandestinely by the garden path and, at once, the whole situation was transformed. Within a few hours the viceroy was safe aboard *La Minerve* with all his luggage and confidential documents, while ashore the 'impossible' evacuation was already under way. The lesson was not lost on an astute man of affairs, 'I like the sea better,' Elliot told his wife. 'The character of the profession is more manly. They are full of life and action, while on shore it is all lounge and still life.'

By now the French were on the move from Leghorn and, on 19 October, their advance force landed on the north coast. However the British evacuation was almost complete and, as the first French troops reached the outskirts of Bastia at dawn on the 20th, Nelson and de Burgh stepped into the last boat and the British force set sail for Elba. He wrote proudly to Fanny,

> The evacuation took place in a manner pleasant to my feelings. Not a creature was left who wished to come off . . . It appeared to others to be a fag to me but I assure you I am never so well pleased to be in active employment, especially when my services are well received by my Commander-in-Chief.

The fort at Bastia, to which General de Burgh and the British troops had already retreated when Nelson arrived to evacuate the town in October 1796.

Nelson and Sir Gilbert Elliot

A cultivated, self-confident and well-educated Scottish aristocrat, some seven years older than Nelson, Elliot (later Lord Minto) was a devoted public servant who, having first entered the Commons at the age of twenty-five, was now pursuing a diplomatic career.

Having originally come out to the Mediterranean as Commissioner for Toulon, he was appointed Viceroy of Corsica once the island fell into British hands in 1794. During the Corsican campaign he came into regular contact with Nelson, for whom he formed a strong admiration that lasted for the rest of his life. Indeed, he became one of Nelson's closest male friends, going so far on one occasion as to claim that 'His friendship and mine is little short of the other attachment [i.e., Emma].' (Minto, vol. III, p. 370.)

In early 1798 his political influence was partly instrumental in obtaining for Nelson the independent command in the Mediterranean, which led eventually to his stunning victory at the Nile.

This comparatively little-known incident demonstrates another key element in Nelson's complex character: his refusal to be weighed down by difficulties. The determination which enabled him to extract the entire British garrison from Bastia, complete with all its valuable equipment, when his Army colleagues considered the task impossible, was the same spirit which led him to ignore Hyde Parker's signal of recall at Copenhagen.

THE RETREAT TO GIBRALTAR

Having landed his charges safely at Porto Ferraio in Elba, Nelson rejoined Jervis at the main British base at San Fiorenzo Bay on the west coast of Corsica to find the whole fleet in a state of anticipation. On 15 October, a large Spanish fleet of nineteen battleships under Langara had appeared off Cape Corse and was assumed to be still in the vicinity. Jervis was still expecting that Man would rejoin him in time and so all seemed set for a major battle. Morale in the British fleet was high. Nelson wrote to Fanny,

> The Dons are coming up but in such a plight that they cannot stand against our fine fleet, when we are all united which I expect we very soon will be. There is nothing our tars look for so earnestly as an opportunity of giving the Dons a total defeat.

In fact, after his brief appearance on 15 October, Langara headed straight for Toulon where he joined with the French ships stationed there on the 26th, thus creating a combined fleet of thirty-four battleships.

Having waited for Man until the last possible moment, Jervis finally sailed with his fleet on 2 November, heading west for Gibraltar and hoping each day to catch sight of his second's sails. But, as the days passed without any sign, doubts began to grow. On 22 November, Nelson sent a chatty note to his friend Collingwood in HMS *Excellent* with a postscript, 'We have reports that Man is gone through the Gut – not to desert us I hope, but I have my suspicions.'

In fact, Man had indeed deserted his colleagues. As he lay at Gibraltar taking on stores, the Spanish fleet sailed eastwards though the Straits. Realizing that they were now between him and his colleagues, he lost his nerve and returned to England, arriving on 30 December. Jervis wrote angrily to Lord Spencer,

> I cannot describe to your Lordship the disappointment my ambition and zeal to serve my Country has suffered by this diminution of my Force; for had Admiral Man sailed from Gibraltar on the 10th October, the day he received my orders, and fulfilled them, I have every reason to believe the Spanish fleet would have been cut to pieces.

The Admiralty agreed: when he arrived at Spithead, Man was ordered to strike his flag and was never employed again.

So, the opportunity for a decisive encounter had been lost and the French and Spanish now had a powerful united fleet at Toulon, while Jervis' force had been reduced to a mere fifteen. Clearly, in the circumstances, he could no longer hope to hold the Mediterranean and, when he arrived at Gibraltar on 1 December, he found orders awaiting him to move his base to Lisbon. But he had one last important task to perform: the rescue of the Corsica garrison, now stranded at Porto Ferraio, in the middle of a hostile sea. It was a delicate operation, requiring both determination and diplomacy, and he had no hesitation in selecting the man to accomplish it. He wrote to Nelson,

> Having experienced the most important effects from your enterprise and ability, upon various occasions since I have had the honour to command the Mediterranean, I leave entirely to your judgment, the time and manner of carrying this critical and arduous service into execution.

It was a handsome compliment from a man who weighed his judgements carefully. Clearly, Nelson was now his most trusted subordinate.

THE ACTION WITH THE *SANTA SABINA*

On 10 December 1796, Nelson left HMS *Captain* and hoisted his pendant in *La Minerve*, commanded by Captain George Cockburn. '[I] . . . am going on an arduous and most important mission which, with God's blessing I have little doubt of accomplishing,' he told Fanny. 'It is not a fighting mission, therefore be not uneasy.' Two days later, he sailed back into the Mediterranean, accompanied by another frigate, HMS *Blanche*.

By Tuesday 19 December the two British frigates were off Cartagena and making good progress towards Elba. Although this was 'not a fighting mission', they were now in a hostile area and so the lookouts were keeping a particularly close watch on the horizon. At about 2220, there came a signal from the *Blanche* that she wished to speak to the commodore. *La Minerve* closed with her consort and Captain D'Arcy Preston explained that he had sighted two ships, presumed to be Spanish. So they cleared for action and set off to investigate, diverging as they went to take on both opponents. They were indeed Spanish: the frigates *Santa Sabina* and *Ceres*.

It is clear from *La Minerve*'s log that Nelson conned the frigate himself during the ensuing action – an unusual course for a flag-officer but not, as we shall see, unusual for him. Two years before, at the Battle of the Gulf of Genoa in March 1795, he had shown his skill as a ship-handler when he manoeuvred his small 64-gun battleship *Agamemnon* to and fro across the stern of the much larger French

> ### The *Santa Sabina* log entry
>
> The entry in *La Minerve*'s log describing the action with the *Santa Sabina* is printed in full by Nicolas (vol. II, pp. 312–3). Unusually long and detailed, running to over 500 words, its use of the first person shows that it was written by Nelson himself. For example, the sighting of the Spanish frigates is reported thus, 'The Captain told me he saw two Spanish frigates to leeward . . . At 20 minutes before 11 I passed under the stern of one of them, which I hailed.'
>
> It was most unusual for a flag-officer to write up a ship's log, so Nelson's action underlines how much importance he attached to the battle – and how anxious he was that it should be reported in the most favourable light.

three-decker, *Ça Ira*, and repeatedly raked her. Now, he demonstrated that skill again and, placing *La Minerve* across the stern of the *Santa Sabina* in a raking position, hailed her and called on her captain to surrender. To his surprise, the answer came back in excellent English, 'This is a Spanish frigate and you may begin as soon as you please', and a furious gun battle erupted. The two foes were fairly evenly matched but darkness gave the edge to the ship with superior training and gunnery and so finally, after refusing several other invitations to surrender, the Spanish commander finally accepted defeat. When he was brought across to *La Minerve* to hand over his sword, the reason for his excellent English was revealed: he was Don Jacobo Stuart, great grandson of King James II. In the meantime, the *Blanche* had tackled the *Ceres* which had put up a much less spirited resistance, surrendering after only seven or eight broadsides.

The battle over, the hard work of repairing damage and securing the prize began. *La Minerve*'s first lieutenant, John Culverhouse took a party across to the *Santa Sabina*, including one of the junior lieutenants, a burly young Dorset man, Thomas Hardy, and a tow rope was secured. Amidst all this noise and bustle, Nelson sat down to write his official report to Jervis. At last, he had won the headline-catching victory for which he longed: he had beaten a powerful enemy in a fair fight. It had been a classic single-ship contest – the sort of action which usually received a separate entry in the *London Gazette* and was commemorated with a popular print. Moreover, the glamour of Don Jacobo's name would give an extra touch of personal interest to the story.

The dispatch he penned, in a noisy ship and after an exhausting battle, was masterly: as he wrote to his father a few days later, 'I may venture to say it was what I know the English like.' He began by giving a brief, sober account of the battle; warmly praised Cockburn and his officers, taking care to mention them all by name (and making no mention of his own involvement with the working of the ship); and concluded with a generous tribute to the gallantry of his opponent.

Scarcely had he finished his letter than he was interrupted. At 0330 another Spanish frigate hove into sight and, ranging alongside the *Santa Sabina*, fired a broadside into her. *La Minerve* cast off her prize, the better to engage this new opponent, which hauled off after a sharp half-hour engagement. More ships were then seen approaching and the growing daylight revealed they were a Spanish squadron of two battleships, accompanied by two frigates. By now, *La Minerve* was badly crippled, with all her masts shot through and her rigging and shrouds slashed. It took all of Nelson and Cockburn's combined skill to escape – helped considerably by the prize crew in the *Santa Sabina* who diverted the attention of the Spanish squadron by hoisting English colours over Spanish. The Spaniards took the bait, abandoned their chase of *La Minerve*, and set about recapturing their former colleague.

The prize crew had sacrificed themselves to let their comrades escape: the sort of action that Nelson never forgot. Culverhouse's future was now assured – as the first lieutenant, he would automatically be promoted as a reward for his part in the capture of the *Santa Sabina* – but Lieutenant Thomas Hardy still had his way to make. From that moment, he was under Nelson's personal protection and became a member of his inner circle of 'followers'.

Nelson was left with a problem: on his desk was a dispatch reporting a decisive victory; but his prize had been recaptured, which meant the victory was now incomplete. With the natural instinct for good public relations that he was to display repeatedly during the rest of his career, he proceeded to make the best of the situation. Instead of tearing up his first letter and starting again, he let the stirring account of the victory stand and wrote a second, and completely separate, letter reporting the recapture of the *Santa Sabina*. The two letters were eventually published together in the *London Gazette* and, as he expected, the letter reporting the victory received the most attention.

THE EVACUATION OF ELBA

So, *La Minerve* continued on her voyage to Elba, arriving as we have already seen, on Christmas morning in time for Nelson to attend General de Burgh's ball as the guest of honour. However, the following day the two men had a more awkward encounter, for de Burgh had not received any direct orders to evacuate Elba and so felt 'uncertain how to act'. Even the news that the Spanish fleet was at large in the western Mediterranean was not sufficient to move him. Sir Gilbert Elliot, whose advice might have swayed the general, was absent on a diplomatic mission to Naples and so Nelson had to resign himself to a further delay. He occupied his

HMS Captain *(centre), flying Commodore Nelson's pendant at her main, lies off Porto Ferraio, following the British capture of Elba on 10 July 1796. Ahead of her is Captain Fremantle's frigate, HMS* Inconstant.

time gathering his ships and arranging for the embarkation of the naval stores, while Captain Thomas Fremantle was sent hurriedly to Naples in the *Inconstant* to fetch the viceroy. With him went the entire Wynne family – still searching for a safe haven in a Europe turned upside down by the remarkable French successes.

In the midst of his activity, Nelson did not forget Culverhouse and Hardy and their prize crew. Determined to release them from Spanish captivity as quickly as possible, he returned Don Jacobo Stuart to his friends in Cartagena bearing two characteristic notes. The first, addressed to the Captain General of Cartagena, made it clear that Don Jacobo would be 'at full liberty to serve his King when Lieutenants Culverhouse and Hardy are delivered to the garrison at Gibraltar' and the second told the Spanish captain's superior, 'I cannot allow Don Jacobo to return to you without expressing my admiration of his gallant conduct.'

It was the kind of courtly, almost romantic, gesture in which Nelson delighted. It was also most effective, for Culverhouse and Hardy were released after only a few weeks in captivity. Nor did Nelson forget the rest of the prize crew: he rounded up all the Spanish prisoners on Elba and sent them off to Cartagena with another note, requesting the immediate release of his men. It was thoughtful gestures such as these that made him beloved.

The *Inconstant* did not return for some time. Elliot was on a tour of the Italian states endeavouring to discover how much support there was for continued opposition to the French and Fremantle was forced to wait for him in Naples. But he did not waste his time. Realizing that he might never see Betsey again, he made a formal offer to Richard Wynne and, with the formidable assistance of the British ambassador's wife, Emma Hamilton, won his prize – with the unexpected addition of a handsome settlement of £8,000. An English service was hastily staged at the British embassy and Emma even managed to procure a blessing from a Catholic priest to satisfy Agathe Wynne – on the understanding that the couple would be married again according to the Roman rite when circumstances permitted. Sir Gilbert Elliot, and his aide Colonel John Drinkwater, arrived in Naples in time to attend the ceremonies and three days later the *Inconstant* set sail for Elba. In her went the viceregal party – and the new Mrs Betsey Fremantle, now embarking on what was to prove a most eventful honeymoon.

When he reached Elba on 22 January, Elliot did not, after all, support Nelson in urging de Burgh to withdraw. The cordial welcome he had received in both Rome and Naples had convinced him it was essential for the British to maintain a naval presence in the Mediterranean and so he considered that Elba should be held at all costs. Nelson still felt bound by his orders from Jervis and so it was decided that only the naval establishment would be withdrawn, leaving sufficient transports to evacuate the troops if required. Meanwhile, Nelson agreed to take Elliot as quickly as possible to Lisbon to consult with Jervis and brief him about the state of affairs in Italy.

So, the viceroy went aboard *La Minerve* and on 29 January she sailed. The convoy bearing the naval supplies headed directly for Gibraltar, escorted by two other frigates, the *Romulus* and *Southampton*. But Nelson had one more duty to perform before he joined his admiral: to find out where the main enemy fleet was located. Setting a more northerly course than his colleagues, he touched first at Toulon where the combined Franco-Spanish fleet had last been sighted some weeks before. The port was empty. Tension mounting, they sailed on down the coast to Cartagena – only to find that too was empty. Clearly, the enemy was at sea and heading for the Straits. The long-expected confrontation was imminent.

✳ ✳ ✳

SOURCES FOR PART ONE

The main source for this section is *The Dispatches and Letters of Lord Nelson* by Sir Nicholas Harris Nicolas. Most of the letters quoted will be found in Volume Two, which starts with a letter from Nelson to his wife from San Fiorenzo in Corsica in January 1795 and ends with a brief note to Lord Spencer, the First Lord of the Admiralty, on 18 December 1798, reporting that his new flagship, HMS *Vanguard*, is ready for service. The main exception to this rule are Nelson's letters to Fanny, all of which are taken from *Nelson's Letters to His Wife* by George Naish.

Other key sources include *The Life and Letters of Sir Gilbert Elliot* by the Countess of Minto; *The Spencer Papers* by J.S. Corbett and *Memoirs of the Right Honourable Lord St Vincent* by J.S. Tucker. A.T. Mahan's *Influence of Seapower upon the French Revolution and Empire* and his magisterial *Life of Nelson* both give a succinct and insightful analysis of the little-known 1796 campaign in the Mediterranean.

The extraordinary story of the Wynne family's flight across war-torn Europe – and their equally remarkable four-month stay with the Mediterranean Fleet – can be found in Volume II of *The Wynne Diaries* edited by Anne Fremantle.

For a vivid visual picture of the events, personalities and places mentioned in this section, together with an excellent series of brief essays based on the latest research, R. Gardiner's *Fleet Battle and Blockade* is highly recommended.

PART TWO

The Battle of Cape St Vincent, 14 February 1797

'My excellent stock.' A commemorative print featuring portraits of Sir John Jervis and all the admirals and captains who served with him at the Battle of Cape St Vincent.

CHAPTER THREE

'In war, much is left to Providence'
The build up to the Battle

'Nothing will be left undone by me.'
Nelson to his wife, 27 January 1797

THE SPANISH ROYAL ARMADA

In mid-January 1796, Teniente General José de Córdoba y Ramos was appointed commander-in-chief of the Spanish fleet in Cartagena. Although he had no previous experience of senior command, he had been given responsibility for Spain's main naval force at a critical moment in the war. More remarkable still, he was the third man to hold the position in six weeks.

Before Spain formally declared war in October 1796, she had taken steps to concentrate her fleet and, as we have seen, nineteen battleships under Langara had entered the Mediterranean at the end of September. Having joined with seven more ships at Cartagena, Langara first cruised off Corsica and eventually reached Toulon on 26 October, where he found twelve French ships. The expedition to Ireland was being planned at that time and so, at the beginning of December, the combined fleets were ordered to sail into the Atlantic. Driving before an easterly gale the French, under Contre Amiral Pierre de Villeneuve, pushed on through the Straits and, having successfully evaded all the British fleets, eventually reached Brest by the end of the year. Although they arrived too late to help in the Irish invasion, they were nonetheless well placed to assist in another, more ambitious, plan to invade Britain from Texel in 1797.

However their Spanish allies were not with them. The voyage to Toulon had demonstrated to Langara that his fleet was far from ready for a major confrontation and he insisted on putting into Cartagena for supplies and repairs, arriving there on 6 December. His stand made him unpopular in Madrid and he was immediately superseded by Teniente General José de Mazarredo. But Mazarredo, who the Spanish naval historian Hugo O'Donnell calls 'one of the most professional of naval officers that Spain had produced since the 16th century', made the same stand as his predecessor, refusing to take command unless the acute problems of supplies and under manning were addressed. As a result, he too was removed and Córdoba appointed.

This undignified game of musical chairs highlights the key weakness in the Royal Armada of Spain at this time. On paper, it was very imposing: with fine ships, an experienced and distinguished officer corps and a call-up system, based on a Sea Registry of the Merchant Navy, that was in advance of any of its rivals. But it was subject to rigid political control from the centre and Chief Minister Manuel de Godoy, a former Guards officer, was no friend to the sea service. The Armada was starved of resources and its more efficient senior officers were discarded if they dared to criticize the minister's policies. One of them, the widely respected Escaño, who had served as Head of the General Staff in the Mediterranean, wrote in 1795,

> . . . it has come to my notice that all the ships, with few exceptions, are in a bad state of repair and without the means to change the situation. Even the weakest of enemies could destroy them with ease . . . If we have to enter into battle this squadron will bring this nation into mourning, digging the grave of the person who has the misfortune to command it.

Scarcely surprising then, that Spain's most senior naval officers declined the poisoned chalice.

The state of the Royal Armada was well known to the British. The two fleets had served together in the early years of the war, when the Spanish weaknesses had been all too apparent. On his way to join the Mediterranean Fleet in June 1793, Nelson called into Cádiz in HMS *Agamemnon* where he was invited to dinner by Langara in his splendid flagship, the *Concepcion*, and allowed to wander freely around the dockyard. His verdict, in a letter to Fanny, was that the Spanish had 'very fine ships but shockingly manned'. He then continued, making what turned out to be a remarkable prophecy,

> I am certain if our six barges' crews (which are picked men) had got on board one of their first rates they would have taken her. Therefore in vain may the Dons make fine ships, they cannot however make men.

As was their custom, his early biographers, the Revd James Clarke and John M'Arthur, edited this letter to make it read more elegantly and omitted the crucial words, 'Therefore in vain', which link the second sentence to what Nelson was

---

The Spanish Royal Armada

British historians have long been aware of the manning and supply problems which the Spanish Royal Armada was encountering. Indeed, some of these problems were highlighted at the time by Drinkwater in his *Narrative* and his material has been included in most earlier British accounts of the battle.

However, the international conference in 1997, 'St Vincent 200', revealed some fascinating new insights, based on the work of a number of Spanish historians – notably, Hugo O'Donnell, José Ignacio Gonzalez-Aller and Agustín Guimerá Ravina – including the extraordinary story, repeated here, of the swift changes in the fleet commander. British readers will find the results of their researches admirably distilled in the papers published in the *St Vincent 200* conference proceedings.

---

saying in the first. Their version persisted and has been quoted in some biographies to show that Nelson was contemptuous of the Spaniards. Now we have the correct version before us, we can see that he was simply making an obvious point: that one cannot 'construct' seamen in the same way as fine ships; they need to be trained by long and hard experience.

Despite their courage, it was experience, above all, that the Spaniards lacked. When Córdoba hoisted his flag in the imposing 130-gun *Santissima Trinidad*, he found that she had only 60 prime seamen in a crew of 900, the rest were landsmen and even soldiers. He had very little opportunity to rectify the situation, or even to discuss tactics with his captains, before he was peremptorily ordered to sea by Godoy. He duly sailed, on 1 February, with 27 battleships, 8 frigates and a flotilla of 28 launches equipped with cannon which were intended to assist with the siege of Gibraltar (for a map of the theatre of operations, see the endpapers).

As if he did not have enough problems, Córdoba was now given an additional task which was to hamper his movements, and lead to disaster, on the day of battle. The Spanish economy depended on the silver imported from the South American colonies and a regular supply of large quantities of mercury was required for its refining. In Málaga, waiting for a safe escort, was a valuable convoy of five ships carrying mercury: four *urcas*, or armed merchant ships, and a man of war, the *Santo Domingo*. Córdoba's orders were to collect these ships on

HMS Victory. *Although this print dates from 1778, it nonetheless gives a good impression of her appearance when she was Jervis' flagship twenty years later. Note the elaborate stern decorations and figurehead, removed in the 'Great Refit' of 1803.*

his way south and to escort them to Cádiz. As so often in naval history, the presence of a valuable convoy was to bring about a decisive battle.

The Spanish reached the Straits by 5 February, where the launches were sent into Alegicras under the escort of three battleships, the *Bahama*, *Neptuno* and *Terrible*, while the rest of the fleet sailed on for Cádiz. The following day they sighted the port and the convoy began to make its way towards the entrance, the warships covering them from the rear. But, at that moment, there was a sudden and severe change of weather: a strong Levanter blew up and Córdoba was forced to ride it out for eight days, being pushed further and further to the west. If he had not been tasked with the safe escort of the convoy it is possible he might have sailed directly north and so missed Jervis completely. But now he had to struggle to stay in a position that would enable him to reach Cádiz with his precious charges, once the wind allowed him to do so. And this enforced halt in his voyage gave Jervis' waiting scouts plenty of time to find him.

FINDING THE SPANISH FLEET

At this point, however, Jervis' fortunes appeared to be at a low ebb. On 10 December an easterly gale in the Straits area had swept three of his battleships from their moorings. HMS *Courageux* struck a rocky headland known as Apes Hill on the Barbary Coast and sank with the loss of almost three-quarters of her crew. Her captain, Ben Hallowell, who had been ashore attending a court martial, suddenly found himself without a ship. The *Gibraltar* and *Culloden* also went ashore but both were refloated, although the former was so badly damaged that Jervis was forced to send her home to England for docking. A few days later, another battleship, HMS *Zealous* struck a rock in Tangier Bay. Jervis' already slender force was therefore reduced to twelve.

Having sent Nelson on his mission to evacuate Elba, Jervis took his remaining ships north to the Tagus, a better position than Gibraltar from which to cover the Straits. But even here, ill-luck pursued him. As the fleet entered the river, on 21 December, HMS *Bombay Castle* struck hard on a sandbank and, after several fruitless attempts to refloat her, had to be abandoned. Then a few days later, HMS *St George* suffered a similar fate and, although refloated, had to return to Lisbon for repairs.

To make matters worse, Jervis was completely in the dark about the whereabouts of the Spanish fleet. He had seen Villeneuve's squadron pass through the Straits on 10 December, driven by the same gale that dispersed his own ships, and assumed that the Spaniards were not far behind. He was worried about Nelson, who he expected would by now be on his way back from Elba with his vulnerable convoy and so, on 18 January, he led his remaining ships to sea to take up a position off Cape St Vincent, 'that will enable me to go speedily to his assistance in case the fleet of Spain should attempt to interrupt his passage through the Gut'.

Adverse winds slowed Jervis' passage considerably and he did not reach his rendezvous until 6 February (the very day that the Spanish sighted Cádiz and were blown out into the Atlantic by the Levanter), where he found a welcome reinforcement of five battleships under Rear Admiral William Parker. They brought with them the news that the Brest fleet had returned to port after its abortive attempt to effect a landing in Bantry Bay. Knowing that his rear was secure, Jervis could now give his whole attention to the approaching Spanish.

But still he had no certain news of them. The latest intelligence from Cartagena, passed on through the Governor of Gibraltar, was that the Spanish fleet was still there and making preparations for sea; but Jervis found this long delay 'incomprehensible' and so he sent ashore for more news. His hunch proved right, for on 9 February the frigate *Viper* arrived from Gibraltar to tell him that the Spanish had passed through the Straits on the 5th. She had sighted them herself the next day, apparently making their way into Cádiz. It seemed that the opportunity had been missed and that the Spanish were once again safely in port.

Then, suddenly, there came a flurry of sighting reports which changed the picture completely. On 10 February, the *Emerald* hailed the *Victory* with the news that the Spanish were still at sea and, from their reported position, it was clear that they had been driven well out into the Atlantic. The next day, the Elba convoy finally arrived safely, escorted by the *Southampton*, and she too had seen the Spanish fleet, reporting that they had obviously suffered badly in the storm and were 'in a good deal of disorder'. This last piece of intelligence decided Jervis: at 1410, he made the signal to prepare for battle and the next morning, 12 February, he led his fleet south-west towards the Spaniards' last reported position. Twenty-four hours later, Nelson finally arrived in *La Minerve*, bringing with him the most complete and detailed report yet received. And, characteristically, it was based not on a distant sighting but on a close personal encounter.

THE VOYAGE OF *LA MINERVE*

Having reconnoitred Toulon and Cartagena, Nelson reached Gibraltar on 9 February only to find that the Spanish fleet had passed through the Straits five days before. He was in a tearing hurry, refusing all invitations to dine ashore: clearly the decisive encounter was imminent and he could not bear the thought that he might miss it. But first Sir Gilbert Elliot had to make his report to the governor and this took time: the commodore's barge was sent to collect him but he failed to turn up and so the frigate missed the tide. The viceroy's private secretary, Edward Hardman, received an impatient note begging him to make sure their party 'will be on board as early in the evening as possible – say eight o'clock – for I will sail the first moment after'. But the delay did have another, more welcome, result: it gave time for Lieutenants Culverhouse and Hardy to be formally exchanged and to rejoin their comrades.

This time, the viceroy and his party arrived punctually and *La Minerve* weighed anchor. As she did so, two Spanish battleships across the bay at Algeciras also got under way, clearly intending to intercept her. For a while the British frigate could make only slow progress in the uncertain wind eddies in the lee of the Rock, while the Spaniards had the advantage of a steady wind, and one of the battleships, the *Terrible*, began to come so close that Elliot began to sort out his most confidential papers in case he needed to throw them overboard.

Nelson, meanwhile, was pacing the deck with Colonel John Drinkwater. The colonel was an acute observer and a keen historian, having already produced an authoritative narrative of the Great Siege of Gibraltar. Many years later, he published a detailed account of the events of the next few days and, although his story has been retold many times, it is worth including again here because of the vivid glimpses it gives us of Nelson in action at this critical period in his career.

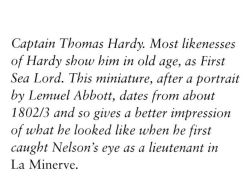

Captain Thomas Hardy. Most likenesses of Hardy show him in old age, as First Sea Lord. This miniature, after a portrait by Lemuel Abbott, dates from about 1802/3 and so gives a better impression of what he looked like when he first caught Nelson's eye as a lieutenant in La Minerve.

As they watched the approaching Spaniard, Drinkwater asked the commodore if an engagement was likely. Nelson replied that it was very possible and then, looking up at his broad pendant, added, 'But before the Dons get hold of that bit of bunting I will have a struggle with them and sooner than give up the frigate I'll run her ashore.' At this point, dinner was announced and Nelson sat down with Elliot and his staff. The party also included the two newly released lieutenants and Drinkwater was just congratulating Hardy on his good fortune when a cry was heard, 'Man overboard!' The officers rushed on deck leaving the civilians to watch the proceedings through the stern windows and, within moments, the jolly boat had been lowered from its davits over the stern and was on its way to the rescue. As it dropped past the windows, Drinkwater noticed that it was commanded by his former dinner partner, Thomas Hardy: once again, the large Dorsetman was showing initiative and quick responses.

Swiftly the little boat fell astern towards the Spaniard. Eventually, Hardy signalled that the man could not be found and his boat's crew began the long row back to their ship. Drinkwater joined Nelson on the quarterdeck and it quickly became apparent that all was not well: the jolly boat was making little progress against the strong current flowing eastwards through the Straits and Hardy was in danger of becoming the guest of the Spaniards once again. Suddenly, Nelson could stand the tension no longer: 'By God, I'll not lose Hardy!' he exclaimed, 'Back the mizzen topsail.' In the heat of the moment, as in the action with the *San Sabina*, he was giving ship-handling orders directly, rather than leaving them to the ship's captain as was customary.

The sail was backed and the frigate slowed down sufficiently for the men in the jolly boat to propel their tiny craft alongside. But this pause also gave the Spanish battleship a chance to catch up and, as the boat was hurriedly hoisted aboard, eyes were trained anxiously astern, expecting any moment to see the first shots fired. Instead, to their amazement, the *Terrible* shortened sail and dropped back to await her consort. Presumably, her captain suspected that Nelson had sighted his own fleet coming down to his aid and did not wish to be caught in a trap. By the time he realized his mistake, *La Minerve* had recovered her boat and was sailing at full speed again. By sunset she had shaken off her pursuers completely.

But the frigate's adventures were not yet over. Later that night, while steering well to the south of the Straits, in order to throw any pursuers off the scent, they found themselves in the middle of a large fleet. It was in fact the main Spanish force, still struggling to get back into Cádiz. Nelson stayed in touch with them, conforming his movements to those of the ships around him, until, in the early hours of the morning, the strange fleet went about and headed northwards. He then set his own course so that he would intercept them if they turned westwards again; but no Spanish ships were sighted. The obvious conclusion was that they were making for Cádiz and so he set off for Jervis' rendezvous at Cape St Vincent to carry this news to the admiral. Meeting up with him at about at 0900 on the morning of 13 February, he went on board the *Victory* to make his report, taking with him, not only Elliot and Drinkwater, but also Culverhouse and Hardy. The two lieutenants were able to give the commander-in-chief first-hand information on the numbers, equipment and discipline of the Spanish fleet, which further confirmed him in his decision to fight them if at all possible.

La Minerve's reconnaissance was a striking demonstration of what a well-trained frigate captain could achieve, even in those days of primitive communications. In the fortnight since he had left Porto Ferraio on 29 January, Nelson had built up a clear and detailed picture of the movements and strength of the Spanish fleet and, by a systematic process of elimination – and his usual good luck – had established their position with some precision.

Later on the 13th, at 1500, came yet another sighting of the Spanish fleet when the *Bonne Citoyenne* reported that they were just 20 miles away to the south-east. When this information was added to all the previous reports, Jervis' task became straightforward. He now knew that the Spanish were to the south of him and moving in an easterly direction: it was therefore certain that they were making for Cádiz. All he had to do to bring about a battle was to set a course that would place him between them and their destination at daylight.

The news spread around the fleet and, as the usual preparations for battle went on, the excitement grew. Nelson returned to HMS *Captain* where he was greeted by Ralph Miller, and by his former first lieutenant, Edward Berry. Although recently promoted to commander, Berry as yet had no ship and was serving on board as a volunteer. Nelson's young protégé, Midshipman William Hoste, later recorded, 'All the officers and men seemed to me to look taller and the anticipation of victory was legibly written on every brow.' Later that afternoon Jervis gave a dinner for Elliot and his staff in the *Victory* at which spirits were high and the closing toast was 'Victory over the Dons in the battle which they cannot escape tomorrow.' Catching the mood, Elliot asked to remain on board the flagship as a volunteer, saying that he had a great desire 'to assist at a general action of the British fleet'. But Jervis was having none of it and the viceroy was packed off to the safety of a frigate, HMS *Lively*. As a small concession, however, the admiral did agree to allow the frigate to stay to watch the approaching battle instead of setting off at once for Britain.

THE FLEETS

As Jervis' dinner guests dispersed, the British fleet was moving into its night-cruising formation of two close-formed columns. There were 15 line-of-battleships: of these, 6 were three-deckers (2 first rates and 4 second rates) and the remaining 9 were all two-decked 74-gunners – apart from the 64-gun *Diadem*.

Over the south-western horizon was a seemingly formidable array of twenty-nine ships. We now know that four of these were the mercury carrying *urcas* which, although well armed and able to defend themselves, were unlikely to play any active role in the battle. Jervis, of course, did not know this and none of the British accounts of the battle give any indication that the *urcas* were identifed. So far as the British were concerned they were warships and they made their judgements accordingly.

Even with these four ships out of the reckoning, the Spanish fleet still appeared a very powerful force. Seven of their battleships were first rates with more than a hundred guns: among them, the famous 'four-decker', *Santissima Trinidad*. In her heyday, the largest ship in the world, she still retained that reputation, although by 1797 she had been overtaken by some of the newer French first rates and her sailing qualities were so poor that she proved a liability in battle. Of the remaining 17 battleships, 2 were 84-gunners and the remainder were all 74s. On paper, therefore, the Spanish had a considerable advantage – a fact that was emphasized in subsequent British accounts of the battle. Contemporary broadsheets and ballads made much of the idea that Jervis was outnumbered almost two to one. In fact, we now know that only twenty-three Spanish battleships actually took part in the battle, which means that the odds were closer to three to two.

This might still seem daunting; but as we have already seen, the Spanish ships were well below their complement of experienced sailors, with large numbers of

---

The Spanish numbers at Cape St Vincent

The 'two-to-one' claims, repeated in most British accounts of the battle, are based on false information about the numbers of battleships actually present in the Spanish fleet during the action. As an appendix to his *Narrative*, Drinkwater reproduced a 'List of the Spanish Line of Battle', found in the *San Ysidro* when she was captured, which gave the names of twenty-seven battleships and most later authorities have adopted this seemingly definitive document.

However, close examination shows that it is inaccurate. It includes the *Neptuno* and *Bahama*, which had been sent into Alegciras on the passage through the Straits, and the *San Pablo* and *Infanta de Pelayo*, which were detached early in the morning of 14 February and did not rejoin until after the battle was over. This left twenty-three battleships to participate in the fighting. The British reports consistently say that there were twenty-seven 'sail of the line' present and, if we subtract from these the four convoy ships, we again arrive at the figure twenty-three. This figure is confirmed by the latest Spanish accounts (see Hugo O'Donnell's paper in the *St Vincent 200* conference proceedings). So, the odds were actually 23:15 (= 1.53:1).

---

soldiers pressed into service as gunners, and they also still lacked essential supplies. On the other hand, the British had a decided advantage both in morale and in training. Ten of their ships had served with Jervis for over a year and had been honed to his high standards of discipline and experience. Although the remaining five, *Prince George*, *Orion*, *Namur*, *Irresistible* and *Colossus*, had joined only a few days previously and so were not used to Jervis' ways, he seems to have had no doubts about their quality, writing to Lord Spencer after the battle,

> I thank you very much for sending me so good a batch as that under Rear Admiral Parker. Had I made the selection I could not be better satisfied . . . they are a valuable addition to my excellent stock.

So, with hindsight, it is clear that the odds against the British were not as high as a simple count of ships and guns would suggest and Jervis' behaviour on the day of battle shows that this is exactly what he thought at the time. As he wrote later, in his official dispatch, his actions were governed by the fact that he was 'confident in the Skill, Valour and Discipline of the Officers and Men I had the Happiness to Command'.

Admiral Sir John Jervis. Most portraits of Jervis were painted when he was an old man and so give a false impression of senility. This earlier likeness captures his distinctive alertness and intelligence: qualities which were well demonstrated at the Battle of Cape St Vincent.

CHAPTER FOUR

'Sir John's well-arranged designs'

The opening stages of the battle

'The more I think of our late action the more I am astonished,
it absolutely appears a dream.'
Nelson to his wife, 28 February 1797

THE COMMANDER-IN-CHIEF

At about 0200 on the morning of 14 February a familiar burly figure was seen ascending the ladder leading to the *Victory*'s quarterdeck. At once, the officers cleared to one side, allowing the admiral to pace alone, broad shoulders slightly stooped, big head constantly turning to catch occasional glimpses of his own ships, ears pricking at the distant thuds of signal guns that told him the Spanish fleet was still drawing near. His personal preparations complete, Sir John Jervis had come on deck to await the dawn.

Jervis was then sixty-four, and had served in the Royal Navy for just over fifty years. A veteran of two major wars, he was an energetic, highly professional officer whose whole life had been dedicated to the Navy – even in peacetime, he made extensive tours of other countries inspecting their naval installations.

A man of rigid personal discipline himself – who, for example, usually rose at two every morning and even then complained he did not have time to deal with all his correspondence – he expected, and exacted, the same degree of commitment from those who served under him. This insistence on high standards often made him appear somewhat stern and unbending and this is the way historians have tended to portray him. But his latest biographers, Emilio Moriconi and Clive Wilkinson, suggest that this traditional view of Jervis is rather superficial and that he was a more complex character than has hitherto been suggested. In particular, they point out that he had a softer, more relaxed side to his nature that is often overlooked. For example, when a sailor under his command spoiled £6 in notes (equivalent to five months' pay) while washing his clothes, Jervis replaced the money out of his own purse.

Jervis' achievement in moulding his fleet into an efficient and well-organized force has always been recognized by historians but he has not enjoyed a high reputation as a fighting admiral. Again, this is unfair: Jervis had won his baronetcy for a successful single-ship action in 1782 and, before arriving in the Mediterranean, had masterminded the naval contribution to the capture of Martinique, one of the most successful combined operations of the Revolutionary War. Throughout this time in command in the Mediterranean his overriding aim was to bring about a decisive battle. He wrote to Lord Spencer on 2 October 1796, 'Be assured I will omit no opportunity of chastising the Spaniards, and if I have the good fortune to fall in with them the stuff I have with me in this fleet will tell.'

THE FLEETS SIGHT EACH OTHER

The day dawned fine but misty. The easterly gale had now given way to breezes from the south-west. They were light, which meant the early morning mists took some time to disperse; and – as would prove significant during the imminent battle – they were also variable and shifting. As the visibility grew Jervis could see that his captains had managed to preserve what he called their 'admirable close order' throughout the night which meant he was starting the day with his fleet already under close command and no time would be wasted in marshalling his forces. He was determined to fight and was heard to say, 'A victory is very essential to England at this moment' – a consideration that was to influence his whole conduct of the battle. As he later put it in his official dispatch:

> . . . judging that the Honor of His Majesty's Arms and the Circumstances of the War in these Seas required a considerable Degree of Enterprize, I felt myself justified in departing from the regular System.

That last phrase is important and needs to be highlighted. Nelson's unorthodox behaviour at the Battle of Cape St Vincent is well known: so well known, indeed, that it has tended to overshadow the important contributions made to the British victory by a number of other participants, most notably Jervis himself. Recent research, based on a careful study of the ship's logs and of all the signals made by Jervis, has established the actual sequence of events with greater clarity than hitherto and it is now clear that Cape St Vincent was an unorthodox battle right from the start. And that unorthodox approach was both initiated and encouraged by Jervis himself (see note on sources on p. 86).

As the grey dawn gave way to full light, the sighting reports began to come in: first of individual ships, from the *Culloden* at 0540, followed by a string of reports from the *Captain* just after 0600. Then at 0706 came the first definite sighting of the enemy fleet from the frigates *Niger* and *Lively* and the sloop *Bonne Citoyenne* was sent to reconnoitre. At 0820 the fleet was ordered to prepare for battle and, as the ships cleared for action, a rich assortment of debris began tossing in the fleet's wake. For example, Peter Bruff, the Master of HMS *Orion*, recorded that they threw overboard large numbers of barrel staves and iron hoops, 'being water casks got up for the use of the ship'; 120 bread bags 'that had been washed and put on the booms to dry' and '250 pieces of pork that was in steep for the ship's company dinner'.

The initial reports seemed to suggest that only a small detachment of the Spanish fleet had been encountered and so at 0920 Jervis ordered his vanmost ships, *Culloden*, *Blenheim* and *Prince George*, to chase them and cut them off. At 0947 the *Bonne Citoyenne* signalled that she saw eight strange sail, so Jervis sent a similar order to the *Irresistible* and *Colossus*. Although not specifically mentioned in the signal, Saumarez in the *Orion* could not resist joining in and Jervis did not order him to be recalled – not the only time that day he was to turn a blind eye to the initiative of a trusted subordinate.

At 1004, *La Minerve* signalled that there were twenty sail, bearing south-west. This was followed at 1030 by the conclusive report, proving that the main Spanish fleet was present, when the *Bonne Citoyenne* signalled 'Strange sail seen are of the line'. As all these signals arrived in the flagship, they were passed on verbally to Jervis by his Captain of the Fleet, Robert Calder, leading to a famous exchange:

'There are eight sail of the line, Sir John.'
'Very well, Sir.'
'There are twenty sail of the line, Sir John.'
'Very well, Sir.'
'There are twenty-five sail of the line, Sir John.'
'Very well, Sir.'

The hesitant Calder persisted: 'There are twenty-seven sail of the line, Sir John,' and, then apparently feeling that his admiral was not responding to the news with sufficient concern, could not resist adding, 'Near twice our own number.' 'Enough sir!' came the sharp rebuke, 'The die is cast and if there are fifty sail I will go through them!' Upon this, Ben Hallowell was quite unable to restrain himself and thumped the admiral on the back approvingly, 'That's right Sir John, that's right,' he exclaimed heartily. 'By God we shall give them a damned good licking!'

This splendid story – first told in 1844 in a biography of Jervis by J.S. Tucker, the son of his secretary, and repeated in every account of the battle since – has obscured the fact that, thanks to the superb reconnaissance of the highly trained

British scouts, the admiral and his staff already knew with some precision how many ships were present in the Spanish fleet. Jervis had been well aware that he was outnumbered when he made his decision to seek a battle two days earlier and he had now carefully manoeuvred his ships during the night into a position from which they could attack on the most advantageous terms. It is likely, therefore, that the scene on the *Victory*'s quarterdeck involved a touch of 'playing to the gallery', a deliberate morale-boosting exercise designed to demonstrate the admiral's confidence and determination.

Now other ships in the fleet were getting their first sight of the enemy. In HMS *Barfleur*, flagship of Vice Admiral the Honourable William Waldegrave, Midshipman George Parsons was at his station alongside the admiral on the quarterdeck. Many years later he recalled how the signal lieutenant, Henry Folkes Edgell, was perched out on the end of the mainyard, peering through the mist. 'I have a glimpse through the fog of their leeward line,' he called down, 'and they loom like Beachy Head in a fog. By my soul they are thumpers!' At that moment, in Parson's words,

> the fog drew up like a curtain and disclosed the grandest sight I ever witnessed. The Spanish fleet, close on our weather bow [i.e., ahead and to starboard] . . . looked a complete forest huddled together; their commander-in-chief covered with signals.

Having ridden out the gale for eight days, Córdoba was now struggling to get his fleet in order. Unlike Jervis, he started the day with very little information about his enemy's numbers or position. An American neutral, who had seen the British before Parker's reinforcement joined, had told him that they had only nine battleships; so, now that he at last had a fair wind for Cádiz, Córdoba was prepared to push through to the port with his precious convoy, even if he had to accept a battle. At dawn his fleet was on an east-south-east course, sailing in three irregular divisions: the rear headed by Morales de los Rios in the *Concepcion*; Córdoba himself leading the centre in the *Santissima Trinidad* and Teniente General Joaquin Moreno in the *Principe de Asturias* heading the van column, and covering the convoy.

At 0800 they heard the English signal guns astern of them as Jervis' scouts reported their sightings; so Córdoba detached two battleships from the rear, the *San Pablo* and *Infanta de Pelayo*, northwards to reconnoitre. They thus became detached from the rest of the fleet and were unable to rejoin until the end of the day. The first British ships were then sighted at 0900 but in a more easterly direction than expected and so, this time, Moreno in the *Principe* was sent to have a closer look. Unaware that the British were very close and about to attack, Córdoba was dispersing his forces when he should have been concentrating them.

At 1000 came the first positive sighting of the English fleet. To Córdoba's dismay it was revealed that there were between fifteen and eighteen battleships and that they were heading directly for him. Clearly it was no longer simply a question of brushing aside a much inferior British force. He now realized that he had a full-scale battle on his hands and so he had to change his plans quickly, with a determined attack developing before his very eyes.

Once again, his actions were largely influenced by the presence of the convoy. Expecting the British attack to fall on his rear, which was the nearest to them, and needing to protect the *urcas* in his van, Córdoba decided to reverse the order of his fleet so that de los Rios's division and his own would be covering Moreno and the mercury ships. He therefore ordered the fleet to come on to the larboard tack, a move which would also enable him to keep the vital weather gauge. These were the signals that young Midshipman Parsons saw from the quarterdeck of the *Barfleur*.

Such a manoeuvre, carried out in the presence of a determined enemy, would have tested the ability of the best-trained fleet. Now the Spaniards' lack of experience showed itself. As they slowly came round on to a north-west heading, the ships began to lose all order and became bunched together, so that they were masking each other's broadsides. Most important, a gap began to open up between the main body of the fleet and the convoy and its immediate escorts, now forming the rear. This meant that Córdoba lost five more battleships from his principal fighting force, the *Principe de Asturias* and *Conde de Regla* (both 112-gunners), *San Firmin* and *Oriente* (74s) and an unnamed 74. His main body was now reduced to eighteen ships, of which one was the mercury-carrying *San Domingo*.

'THE ADMIRAL MEANS TO PASS THROUGH THE ENEMY'S LINE'

Seeing the gap opening up, Jervis realized that he had been given a marvellous opportunity. As we have seen, he was not aware of the presence of the mercury ships. So, as he looked to the south-east, he saw only what appeared to him to be a division of nine warships that was now detached from the main body. If he could keep them separated from their colleagues he would reduce the odds against him considerably. Accordingly, at 1057, he made his first unorthodox order of the day: the fleet was to form line of battle on a south-south-west heading, ahead and astern of the flagship 'as most convenient' – in other words, without wasting time by waiting to form up in the prearranged order of battle. Then, at 1126, came the crucial signal, 'The admiral means to pass through the enemy's line.' This was not to be a formal battle in the old style: in his desire to catch his enemy off guard Jervis was 'departing from the regular system' right at the outset.

So unexpected was this sudden decision to attack that even some of his own ships were taken by surprise. In the *Colossus*, for example, part of the ship's company had just been piped to dinner and, as the drums beat to quarters sending the men rushing to their guns, a cask containing 58 gallons of wine had to be hove overboard.

The British line of battle at Cape St Vincent

The British ships scrambled into line with no regard for any prearranged order. As a result, it is difficult to find two plans which agree on the correct order and most of those published clash in some particular with contemporary accounts of the battle.

The order shown in Plan I on p. 48, and used throughout this account, is taken from a list headed 'British Line of Battle *as Formed*' (my italics) which appears in a 'Biographical Memoir of John Jervis, Earl of St Vincent', published in the *Naval Chronicle*, vol. IV, p. 38. Although this order differs from all the other available plans, it derives from a reliable source. Moreover, we know that the *Chronicle* editors usually assembled the biographical material by applying directly to their subject, so the list may well have been supplied by Jervis himself.

The same order appears in the caption to a print of the opening stages of the battle, published in June 1797 by Boydell and based on a sketch by Lieutenant Jaheel Brenton who served in HMS *Barfleur*. For a full rehearsal of all the evidence see my article, 'Reconstructing the British Line of Battle at Cape St Vincent', *Nelson Dispatch*, vol. 6, Part 2, pp. 55–7.

However, as soon as the admiral's intentions became clear, the British fleet entered into the spirit of the occasion, swooping down on their opponents 'like a hawk to his prey', as Collingwood later vividly described it to his wife. As the great ships jostled for position in the quickly forming line, there were some scenes reminiscent of Shakespeare: for example, as the *Captain* pushed into place astern of Waldegrave's *Barfleur*, young George Parsons heard his Captain, James Dacres, hail the 74 'to say that he was desired by the vice admiral to express his pleasure at being supported by Sir Horatio Nelson'.

As Jervis had intended, this rapid formation of the British line of battle, in itself a remarkable corporate feat of seamanship and ship-handling, threw Córdoba off balance. He had expected to have more time to make his preparations and he later acknowledged that the speed of the British deployment was one of the reasons for his defeat:

> . . . they formed in regular order of battle, and so near as to oblige my forming the line hastily, without attention to posts, or to the consequences that might result from this bad position of the ships and commanders.

'Supported by Sir Horatio Nelson'

George Parsons wrote his memoirs, *Nelsonian Reminiscences*, many years after the event, in 1843, and so historians have tended to dismiss this charming story as an old man's embellishment. After all, he not only anticipates Nelson's knighthood by a few weeks but, more seriously, for his story to work it is necessary for the *Barfleur* to be close to the *Captain* in the line of battle; whereas in the traditional order she is usually shown further up the line, directly astern of the *Victory*.

It now seems likely that the *Barfleur*'s place in the line was in fact exactly where Parsons says it was (see Plan I on p. 48), so we can now reclaim his story with some confidence and add it to the St Vincent narrative.

It was now a race to see if the leading British ship, Troubridge's *Culloden*, could reach the gap before Moreno in the *Principe* could close it. For some moments it looked as if a collision was inevitable, but when Troubridge's first lieutenant pointed this out, his captain retorted, 'Can't help it Griffiths, let the weakest fend off!' The two ships passed so close that the *Culloden*'s crew could see their opponents through the open gun ports and then a murderous double-shotted broadside, followed swiftly by a second, forced the *Principe* to veer away, her sides visibly shuddering with the impact of the hail of shot.

So, thanks to Troubridge's iron nerve, the British had won the first critical encounter of the battle and Jervis had achieved his first aim: to divide the Spanish fleet. He now had to ensure that the fleet remained divided, so he kept his line on its south-south-west course for another twenty minutes, creating an impenetrable wall of ships between the two Spanish divisions. He has been criticized by those who believe he should have turned his line at once to deal with the main body of the Spaniards to the north-west. But this armchair criticism does not allow for the fact that the smaller leeward Spanish division to the south-east still appeared to pose a considerable threat. We know that there were only five warships in that group; but for Jervis they were a significant force and he had to be certain they had been cut off before he turned to deal with the main body of Spaniards.

By 1200, he was satisfied that his line had advanced far enough to prevent the two Spanish divisions from rejoining and felt he could now put into effect the second part of his plan: an attack in force on the main Spanish body. Accordingly, at 1208 he gave the order for his ships to tack in succession. Anticipating such a move, Troubridge had already ordered the acknowledgement to be bent on a stop

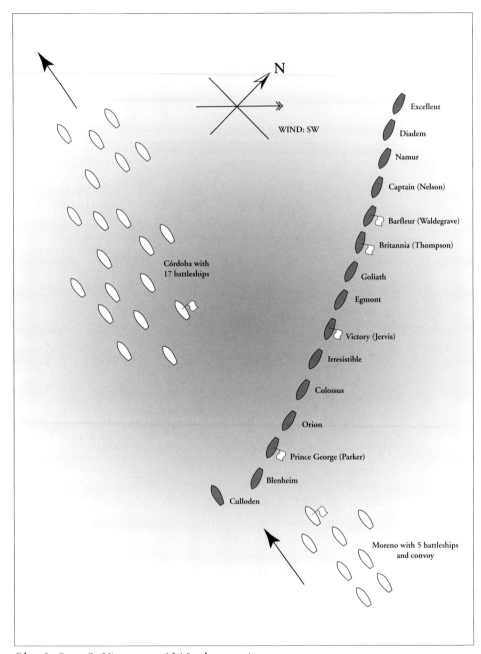

N

WIND: SW

Excellent

Diadem

Namur

Captain (Nelson)

Barfleur (Waldegrave)

Britannia (Thompson)

Córdoba with
17 battleships

Goliath

Egmont

Victory (Jervis)

Irresistible

Colossus

Orion

Prince George (Parker)

Blenheim

Culloden

Moreno with 5 battleships
and convoy

Plan I: Cape St Vincent, c. 1210: the opening stages.

Rear Admiral Sir Thomas Troubridge. Troubridge was one of Jervis' special favourites and this print is taken from a portrait that was in the old admiral's own collection. He is wearing the St Vincent medal on his left lapel, above the one for the Nile.

at the masthead. As soon as the admiral's signal was reported to him, he shouted, 'Break the stop. Down with the helm!' and within minutes the *Culloden* had spun round and was heading north-west towards the main Spanish fleet (see Plan I opposite). 'Look Jackson!' cried Jervis in delight, to his sailing master in the *Victory*,

> Look at Troubridge there! He tacks his ship to battle as if the eyes of England were upon him; *and would to God they were*! for then they would see him to be, as I know him, and, by heavens, Sir, as the Dons will soon feel him!

THE SPANISH LEE DIVISION ATTACKS

Thus far superior seamanship, and Jervis' rigorous training, had enabled the British to win all the points: Colonel Drinkwater, who with Sir Gilbert Elliot was watching the unfolding drama from the quarterdeck of the *Lively*, later wrote that the fleet manoeuvred as if it was performing at a fleet review. But now the first important test of their mettle was materializing. By ordering his fleet to tack 'in succession' (that is, one after the other) Jervis was taking a significant risk. Such a manoeuvre meant that each of his ships would turn at exactly the same spot and any square-rigged warship was particularly vulnerable at the moment of tacking. An obvious counter for an opponent was to concentrate on the turning point: and this is exactly what the Spanish now did, thus setting in motion the second phase of the battle.

As Rear Admiral Parker's flagship, HMS *Prince George*, third in the line, made her turn at about 1230, one of her lieutenants, Thomas Bond, noticed that 'some of the lee division of the enemy had tacked and were standing towards us'. Moreno, in the 112-gun *Principe*, was preparing to mount a determined attack with his four consorts. The *Prince George*'s next astern, Saumarez's *Orion*, got round safely but by now the Spaniards were within close range and, as the *Colossus* began to go about, a shot severed the slings securing her foreyard which fell, taking with it her fore-topsail yard. The sudden loss of her head sails caused her to swerve sharply and miss stays. The *Principe* closed in for the kill, her crew already preparing a line to take the *Colossus* in tow, but Saumarez backed the *Orion*'s maintopsail and covered his consort with his broadsides as she dropped out of the line. The *Principe* wore and the next British ship, *Irresistible*, fired four quick broadsides into her.

Now the *Victory* was approaching, her crew cheering their comrades in the *Colossus*, who were struggling to clear away the wreckage as she drifted away to the north. As the British flagship reached the turn, Moreno's division made another attack, the *Principe* leading, so the *Victory*'s maintopsail was backed, stopping her right in the Spaniard's path. The *Principe* was forced to turn away hurriedly, thus exposing herself to two massive broadsides that caused great damage to ship and crew alike.

Still Moreno had not given up. The *Victory*'s next astern, the *Egmont*, was fired on by the two three-deckers and, as the *Goliath* approached, she found the *Principe* and the *Conde de Regla* waiting for her, this time hove to in raking positions. But, as her log records, she gave them 'a brisk fire' and made her turn successfully, although her rigging was badly shot about and eight men wounded by the Spanish broadsides.

For some reason, these repeated attempts by Moreno's division to break the British line – which are fully documented in the logs of the various British ships involved – have been omitted from earlier accounts of the battle, some of which are fairly contemptuous of the actions of the leeward division. In fact, as Nelson himself later bore witness, Moreno 'did everything which a good officer could do, to attempt to cut through the British line'.

These successive repulses of determined attacks – a classic demonstration of the power of a well-ordered line of battle – finally convinced Moreno that he would not break the tight British formation. Just before 1300, therefore, he gave up the attempt and began a long beat westwards against the wind, intending to reunite with the main body by making his way round the southernmost end of the British line. The *Oriente* was unable to follow him and she made her way down the lee of the British line, exchanging distant fire as she went. The second critical encounter of the battle had been decided – once again in favour of the British.

SIR JOHN ENCOUNTERS DIFFICULTIES

So, as the *Victory* came out of her turn at about 1245, Jervis could feel well pleased with himself. He had split the Spanish fleet and repelled a very spirited attack by their rear, driving it out of the battle. Now he was free to concentrate all

The Victory *in action at Cape St Vincent. HMS* Victory *(centre), supported by Admiral Waldegrave's flagship HMS* Barfleur *(right), fires a broadside into the stern of the* Salvador del Mundo.

his attention on the main body of the Spanish fleet without worrying that the other Spaniards might attack him in the rear.

However, Moreno's gallant action had succeeded in holding up the British long enough to give the Spanish main body a chance to escape. As Jervis now looked to the north-west, where Troubridge in the *Culloden*, followed by the rest of the van, was within a few hundred yards of the rearmost Spanish ships, he could see that a large gap had now opened in his own line, caused by the accident to the *Colossus* and the *Victory*'s own halt to deal with the *Principe*. Instead of a complete line of battle he now had two unequal divisions, separated from each other by at least half a mile (see Plan II on p. 57).

Moreover the wind, which had been backing all morning, had now shifted two full points so that it was blowing from west-south-west. This was forcing the ships astern of the *Victory* to head on a more southerly course, thus further increasing the gap between them and the ships in the van. Instead of being able to concentrate his whole force on the main Spanish body, as he had hoped to do, there was now a grave danger that his five vanmost ships might be cut off and captured.

The third phase of the battle was now developing and if Jervis made the wrong decision the Spanish might yet escape without serious loss – or even inflict losses on him.

Wrestling with this new set of circumstances, Jervis climbed the ladder to the *Victory*'s poop, presumably hoping that the added height would enable him to see over the smoke that was enveloping his flagship. But this was a very exposed position and, as he stood there, a cannon shot from Moreno's division smashed the head of a seaman standing nearby, covering the admiral in brains and blood. Captain Grey rushed up with anxious enquiries, fearing the worst. 'I am not at all hurt,' replied Jervis, calmly, wiping his mouth with a handkerchief, 'But do, George, try if you can get me an orange.' A midshipman ran up with one and Jervis rinsed his mouth with it as he considered his next step.

The orthodox response would have been either to order his van to withdraw (as, for example, Admiral Hotham had done in similar circumstances at the Battle of Hyères in June 1795), or to tell them to heave to and wait for their comrades to catch up. But Jervis was not working by the rulebook; he was still searching for a way to bring about a decisive engagement. Returning to the quarterdeck at about 1250, he gave two orders. The first, to his sailing master, was to alter course slightly to port on to a north-west heading. Since the Spanish were heading north-

---

'Do, George, try if you can get me an orange.'

The story of Jervis' sang-froid on the poop deck has been retold many times and, as so often in such cases, it has become garbled. Jervis' biographer, J.S. Tucker (whose father was the admiral's secretary and was in the *Victory* at St Vincent), said that it was a Royal Marine whose blood and brains bespattered the admiral and all subsequent accounts have followed him. But the *Victory*'s casualty list shows that she suffered only one fatality – and he was a seaman.

Additionally in some versions (including, it has to be admitted, one by the present author!), an odd quirk of Chinese whispers has transformed the officer who came to Jervis' aid into a Royal Marine captain – which means that Jervis commits the solecism of calling a junior Royal Marine officer by his Christian name.

In fact, of course, the man who rushed up to the apparently stricken admiral was the *Victory*'s commanding officer – Captain George Grey.

north-west, and his own van north by west, it seems clear that what he intended to do was to lead his own centre division to windward of the Spanish, thus doubling on their line and catching them between two fires.

The second order, to his flag lieutenant, was for two signals. The first, made specifically to HMS *Britannia*, flagship of Vice Admiral Sir Charles Thompson commanding the rear division, was for the 'leading ship to tack and others in succession'. The second, to all ships, was 'to take up suitable stations for mutual support and engage the enemy as arriving up in succession'. Putting these two signals together, it seems clear that Jervis intended his whole rear division (i.e., the *Britannia* and the five ships astern of her) to tack at once and reinforce the van without waiting to reach the original turning point. In other words, he was now abandoning his single line of battle and was dividing his fleet into three separate divisions which were to act independently. The rear division was to get into action as quickly as possible to support the van and prevent it from being overwhelmed; while he himself, with the centre division, caught up with the Spanish from the rear.

This was a complicated concept to convey by signal – especially in view of the limitations of eighteenth-century communications at sea. There was no signal in the book that stated exactly what Jervis intended; nor did the system enable him to construct a special signal to suit the circumstances. He was therefore forced to select signals which came as close as possible to saying what he wanted, trusting in his subordinates' ability to read the message intelligently, and to understand what their admiral was trying to tell them to do.

So the flags were hoisted and Jervis and his officers watched anxiously for the acknowledgement to be flown in the *Britannia* and for the manoeuvre to begin. But, as the vital minutes ticked past, the big three-decker continued sailing southwards on her original course, followed by her division. The reason for her failure to carry out Jervis' order has never been fully explained. According to her log, her jib-boom had been shot away at about 1230 and it is possible that this damage made it difficult for her to tack. On the other hand, the log does not mention the signal, so it is possible they simply did not see it. Certainly, Jervis was never again happy with Vice Admiral Thompson and did all he could to get rid of him, which suggests he was dissatisfied with his behaviour in the battle.

The *Britannia*'s failure to change course meant that with every minute that passed Jervis' van was becoming more and more exposed. The *Culloden* at last reached the two rearmost Spanish ships and opened fire at about 1300; her next astern, the *Blenheim* about ten minutes later; and unless they could be quickly reinforced, their situation would be perilous in the extreme. It was the third critical moment of the battle, indeed the most critical of all, when the whole issue hung delicately in the balance. And it was at this point that Nelson made his famous intervention.

Boarders away! Most contemporary depictions of Nelson's famous feat in boarding two Spanish ships at Cape St Vincent are rather sanitized. By contrast, this pen and wash drawing by William Bromley captures vividly the brutality of the fierce hand-to-hand fighting.

CHAPTER FIVE

'Nelson's Patent Bridge for Boarding First Rates'
The climax of the battle

'Sir John Jervis is immortalised and Commodore Nelson a hero beyond Homer's.'
Sir Gilbert Elliot to his wife, 1 March 1797

NELSON JOINS THE VAN

HMS *Captain*, flying Nelson's broad pendant, was stationed in the rear of the British line and from her deck Nelson had a grandstand view of the battle as it unfolded. It was his first full-scale fleet action and he was watching with a connoisseur's eye what he later called 'Sir John's . . . well-arranged designs on the Enemy'.

At about 1250 (he later said 1300, but the *Captain*'s time was ahead of the *Victory*'s) he saw, and duly noted, Jervis' two signals ordering the British rear into action. But then, at almost the same moment, something far more arresting caught his attention. Glancing across at the main body of the Spanish fleet, he saw their heads begin to turn and realized that they were changing direction towards him.

By now, the headmost ships in the main Spanish body were well clear of the British rear. Spotting this, Córdoba made a series of signals designed to manoeuvre his force eastwards around the last British ship to join up again with his convoy. These signals were seen only by a small group close to his flagship but, as they all turned eastwards in response, their concerted movement caught Nelson's eye.

Quickly, he summed up the situation. Looking south to the *Victory*, he could see that she was partially obscured by gunsmoke and so he assumed she was still in action and that Jervis was probably too preoccupied to spot what the Spanish were doing. Closer to him, he could see that the *Britannia* had failed to obey the commander-in-chief's signal and was still sailing southwards towards the original turning point. In any case, he realized that Jervis' new order for the rear division to tack *in succession* (rather than all together) was inappropriate to the situation that was now developing; for, if the ships all waited for their next ahead to turn, the Spanish movement eastwards would be given time to mature into a serious threat.

So, in the act of inspired initiative that has rightly won him universal praise, he decided on what he himself called a 'prompt and extraordinary measure'. Ignoring the 1250 signal to tack in succession, he gave the order, instead, for the *Captain* to wear. In other words, she was to turn away from the wind – a quicker manoeuvre than tacking, which involved turning into it. First the ship's bows swung to port – away, that is, from the main Spanish force. But she continued to turn in a wide 270° arc until she was pointing directly towards them and then, having dodged through the British line just ahead of the rearmost ship, Collingwood's *Excellent*, she set off alone to reinforce Troubridge and his colleagues in the van. It was only a short distance to cover, perhaps as little as a mile, and so she arrived in the thick of the action at about 1310. (See Plan II opposite.)

It was a highly risky manoeuvre. As the *Captain* sailed alone towards the Spanish she presented a clear target to the guns of at least five heavily armed ships. But, as Nelson no doubt calculated, the gunnery of those ships was not very accurate, while, on the other hand, the *Captain*'s guncrews had been rigorously trained by Ralph Miller. The addition of their rapid, well-aimed broadsides to those of the *Culloden* turned the tide of the battle decisively in the British favour. Thrown off balance by this sudden onslaught from two highly trained ships and seeing the rest of the British van coming up fast behind them, Córdoba abandoned his move to the east around the British rear and resumed his north-west course. As Miller later put it in a letter to his father (see Appendix 1), the whole Spanish fleet had been turned 'as two shepherd's dogs wou'd a flock of sheep'. The third critical moment of the battle had been won by the British.

As Nelson expected, his initiative was approved by his commander-in-chief. In the *Victory* the maladroit Calder spotted what was happening and, clearly out of touch with the spirit of this remarkable battle so unlike anything he was used to, said to Jervis, 'Sir, the *Captain* and *Culloden* are separated from the fleet. Shall I recall them?' 'I will not have them recalled,' snapped Jervis, 'I put my faith in those ships. It is a disgrace that they are not supported and [are] separated.' Our source for that story is Nelson himself, in a letter to his brother written almost two months after the battle and it is likely that the last sentence is a Nelsonian embellishment. He was convinced that he and Troubridge had fought alone whereas, as we will see, they were supported by at least four other ships. But the rest of the dialogue has an authentic ring (see note on p. 78).

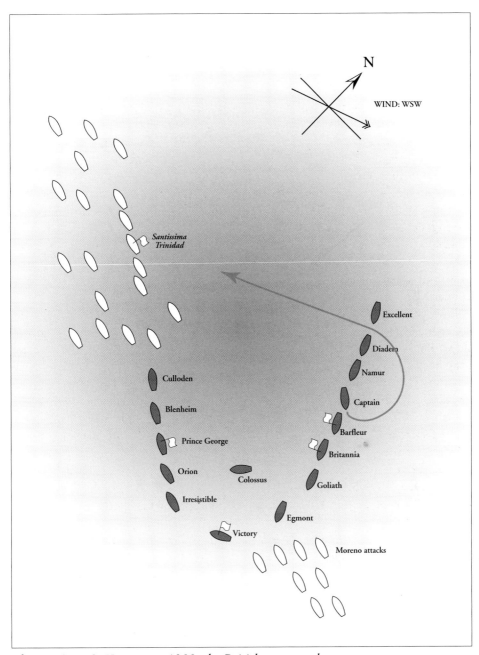

Plan II: Cape St Vincent, c. 1300: the British van attacks.

The significance of Nelson's action

To understand the significance of what Nelson did, it is important to appreciate that Jervis made two separate signals to tack during the battle: one at 1208 to the whole fleet and the other at 1250 to the rear division alone. Nelson mentioned only the second signal in his account and so, unwittingly, misled historians – many of whom have conflated the two signals and based their assessment of the battle on the mistaken assumption that Nelson wore out of the line at the same time as the *Culloden* tacked. In fact, the two events were forty minutes apart.

As a result of this often-repeated mistake, Nelson's move has been misunderstood in the past: being portrayed as an act of disobedience, involving considerable professional risk because he left the 'sacred' line of battle and, moreover, risk to his ship because he took on the entire Spanish fleet alone (for the classic expression of this view, see Warner, pp. 107–8). Modern research, based on a careful analysis of the logs of the ships involved, and of Jervis' signals, has qualified this judgement considerably.

First, by 1300 the British line was already fragmented; and Jervis had in any case just initiated a break-up of the line ahead formation by ordering his centre and rear to act independently. So, the single, rigid line of battle had already been abandoned.

Second, Nelson did not take on the Spanish alone. Rather, he took his place at the head of the British van, just in front of the *Culloden* which had begun engaging the Spanish centre about ten to fifteen minutes earlier.

Third, although Nelson certainly acted on his own initiative, his move to join his colleagues in the van was entirely within the spirit of the orders that Jervis had just given: the admiral had signalled his rear to reinforce his van and that is what the commodore did.

So, 'disobedience' is not an appropriate word to describe Nelson's action: it is more helpful to see it as another demonstration of the remarkable degree of understanding and trust which had grown up between the two men.

THE ATTACK ON THE MAIN SPANISH DIVISION

The Spanish fleet was by now thoroughly disorganized and, without a strong line of battle, each individual ship was vulnerable to the wolves that were now beginning to snap at their heels. The attempt to move to the east, and subsequent return to the original course, had wasted valuable time and the ships of the British

---

Jervis' approval of Nelson's manoeuvre

A document acquired recently by the Royal Naval Museum's archive reinforces the view that Nelson's initiative was entirely in line with the way Jervis wished his individual captains to act.

It is a copy of Jervis' first sailing orders for the Mediterranean Fleet, issued on 4 December 1795, only a few days after he had taken up his new command. In it, he instructs his two smallest and fastest battleships, the *Diadem* and the *Agamemnon* (then commanded by Nelson), to act independently: 'they are at liberty to take any advantage of the Enemy, beaten or disabled (which may appear to them practicable) *without waiting for a signal from the Admiral*' (my italics). (RNM 1990/290)

Furthermore, Jervis reinforced his approval of Nelson's manoeuvre by incorporating it into his planning for future battles. On 28 March 1797, he issued two memoranda to the fleet explaining his tactical thoughts. They were accompanied by six diagrams – one of which plainly shows the British fleet breaking through an enemy line in the same formation as at Cape St Vincent. The vanmost ship has just tacked – and, simultaneously, the rearmost ship has also turned to engage the enemy. (The Navy Records Society, *Naval Miscellany*, vol. II, p. 301.)

---

van were now coming up fast and threatening the rearmost Spanish ships. It was also obvious that the British were beginning to concentrate on the *Santissima Trinidad* and, to counter this, at about 1400 Córdoba hoisted signal 252, 'Each unit should enter the combat as soon as it can', in an attempt to bring his unengaged ships into the action. But the signal was hoisted on the flagship's mizzenmast, so it could not be easily seen by the vanmost ships, at which it was chiefly directed. Worse, those who did see it, did not understand the order, considering it 'impossible that the General would order an attack in disorder'. At the same time, Córdoba struggled to form a protective line, using the ships immediately around him: the *Mexicano* formed on the *Trinidad*'s bow and the *San José*, *San Nicolas*, *Soberano* and *Salvador del Mundo* astern.

It was not a moment too soon, for by then the rest of the British fleet was poised to make an attack in force. At 1319, realizing that the *Britannia* was not going to comply with his earlier signal, Jervis signalled a direct order to the entire rear division to come on to the larboard tack. At this, all the remaining ships in the rear moved individually to join the fray, finding themselves a place wherever they could. Their methods varied according to the sailing qualities of the vessels.

Collingwood's movements

Most accounts of the battle say at this point that Jervis specifically ordered Collingwood to go to Nelson's aid as soon as he saw what the *Captain* was doing. Examination of the logs of the *Victory* and the *Excellent* shows that no such signal was made. Instead, for an hour or so, Collingwood acted in close support of his admiral – and so was at least half a mile away from his old friend.

Once again, as with Nelson's earlier action, the mistake has originated because of a misreading of the signals. At about 1415 (see p. 63), Jervis did indeed order the *Excellent* to 'pass through the enemy's line' – that is, to join the *Captain* and the other ships in the van – but this was more than an hour after Nelson had made his impetuous move.

For example, the *Barfleur* followed Nelson's example and wore. Being a fast sailer, she was able to get into position directly astern of the *Victory*, where she remained for the rest of the action. The *Britannia* and *Namur*, both rather heavy sailers, eventually managed to reach the rear of Jervis' own column – but were only actually engaged right at the end of the action. The smaller and much handier *Diadem* joined the rear of Admiral Parker's van division, where she was a valuable reinforcement in the contest that was fast developing. The rearmost British ship, Collingwood's *Excellent*, fell in ahead of the flagship and led Jervis' line, which was still diverging from the van division, so as to take the Spanish on their hitherto disengaged windward side.

Thus, by 1345, a ferocious mêlée was in progress as ship after ship of the British fleet caught up with the rearmost Spanish ships (see Plan III opposite). The flagship was flying the signal that Nelson was later to make his own trade mark, 'Engage the Enemy More Closely!'; but the order was so well obeyed that, at 1435, Jervis was forced to signal the *Diadem* and *Irresistible* in his leeward line to cease firing, since their shot was falling uncomfortably near the *Victory* and *Excellent* in the windward line.

Meanwhile, further to the north and leeward, the van ships were still hotly engaged with the Spanish centre, including the *Trinidad* and her protecting consorts – especially the two next astern, the *San Nicolas* and *San José*. As the attack developed, Parker ordered his ships to, 'Fill and stand on' (i.e., to fill their sails and move further up the Spanish line) so as to make room for the ships coming up astern of him, a manoeuvre which took first the *Blenheim*, and then the *Prince George* and *Orion*, ahead of the *Captain* in a leapfrogging movement.

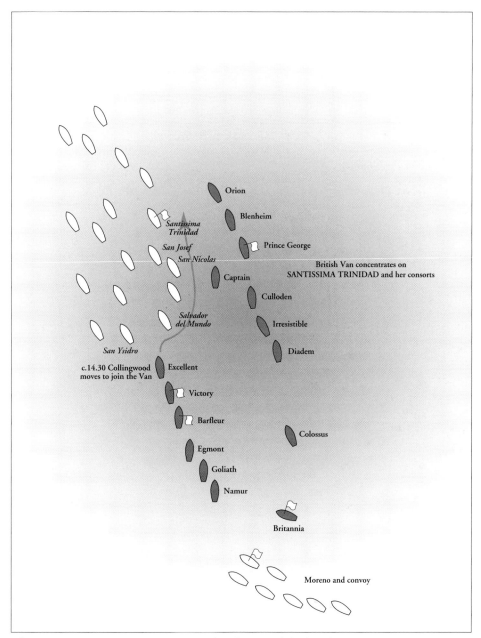

Plan III: Cape St Vincent, c. 1400: the climax of the battle.

By now, Córdoba realized that his fleet was in grave danger. Just as earlier he had been caught off guard by the speed with which the British had formed their line and exploited the opportunity offered by the gap in his fleet, so now he was disconcerted by the ferocity of their attack. As he said in his dispatch, the way in which they fought, 'in great good order, with a heavy and well-directed fire, decided the action in their favour'. Drinkwater, watching from the deck of the *Lively* gained the same impression:

> Advantage was now apparent in favour of the British Squadron . . . The superiority of the British fire, and its effects on the enemy's hulls and sails, were so evident, that we in the frigate no longer hesitated to pronounce a glorious termination of the contest.

The fourth phase of the battle was developing and the fourth – and ultimately decisive – critical moment was imminent.

It was now the turn of Cuthbert Collingwood in HMS *Excellent* to show his mettle. Both the *Captain* and *Culloden* were in some danger. Their rigging was

The other heroes of Cape St Vincent. Nelson's exploits have overshadowed the achievements of his colleagues, notably Captain James Saumarez of HMS Orion *(left) and Captain Cuthbert Collingwood of HMS* Excellent *(right). In these engravings, both based on portraits painted after they had reached flag rank, they are proudly wearing their St Vincent medals in their left lapels.*

severely shot up and the *Captain* had lost her fore-topmast and wheel, so that she could not manoeuvre easily and the powerful Spanish ships to which they were opposed were putting up a spirited resistance. Seeing that the two British ships needed further reinforcement, Jervis signalled at 1415 to the *Excellent* to 'pass through the enemy line'; upon which Collingwood moved from his position ahead of the *Victory* and, setting more sail, got among the rearmost Spanish ships. He first encountered the 112-gun *Salvador del Mundo* into which he poured a series of well-aimed broadsides at close range. As he later told his wife,

> we were not farther from her than the length of our garden. Her colours came down, and her fire ceased. I hailed and asked if they surrendered; and when by signs made by a man who stood by the colours I understood that they had, I left her to be taken possession of by somebody behind and made sail for the next but was very much surprised on looking back to find her colours up again and her battle re-commenced.

The *Excellent* now encountered the *San Ysidro*, a 74, and Collingwood's letter continued, 'Our fire carried all before it, and in ten minutes she hauled down her colours; but I had been deceived once and obliged this fellow to hoist English colours before I left him.' At 1453, he signalled to the *Victory*, 'The enemy's sternmost ship not secure' and Jervis ordered the frigate *Lively* to take possession of the first British prize; thus giving Sir Gilbert Elliot and Colonel Drinkwater a grandstand view of the remarkable climax of the battle that was unfolding.

Collingwood, having made sure of the *San Ysidro*, was soon on the move again, 'with all my ragged sails set'. At about 1500 he passed between the *Captain* and the *San Nicolas* and *San José*:

> . . . we did not touch sides, but you could not put a bodkin between us, so that our shot passed through both ships, and in attempting to extricate themselves they got on board of each other. My good friend, the Commodore, had been long engaged with these ships, and I happily came to his relief, for he was dreadfully mauled.

Out of control, the two Spanish ships smashed into each other and Collingwood moved on yet again, heading for the looming bulk of the *Santissima Trinidad*, potentially the most valuable prize of all and for which, as he later told his brother, 'I had an envious longing.'

NELSON AND HIS BOARDING PARTY

In the shattered *Captain*, the ship's company took advantage of the brief respite to replenish their empty shot lockers and repair the rigging, which had been badly cut about by the concentrated fire of the *Santissima Trinidad* and her consorts.

'Nelson's Patent Bridge for Boarding First Rates.' As her crew climb along the bowsprit, ready to board, HMS Captain *ranges alongside the* San Nicolas. *The bows of the* San José *can be seen beyond the* San Nicolas.

She had also suffered a number of casualties, including Nelson himself, who had been struck in the side by a splinter from one of the rigging blocks and would have fallen if Miller had not been at his side to catch him. 'I was shockingly alarmed at the idea of losing him,' wrote Miller to his father, 'just as his gallantry had won my esteem and affection as much as twenty years acquaintance under tamer circumstances.'

Most men, having dared so much with such brilliant success and having now been rescued from almost certain destruction, would have rested on their laurels – but such was not Nelson's way. Indeed, his finest moment was still to come. Seeing that the crew of the *San Nicolas* was still reeling from the shock of the *Excellent's* broadsides and were now preoccupied in struggling to free their ship from the *San José*, he realized that he had been given a perfect opportunity. And once again he acted with promptness and courage. Ordering Miller to take the *Captain* alongside the stricken Spaniard, he called for boarders and placed himself at their head.

This instinctive act of leadership is so famous that it is easy to forget just how unusual it was for a flag-officer, however junior, to lead a boarding party in person. Indeed as the *Captain* ranged alongside her prey, her bow ramming into the Spaniard's starboard quarter and her spritsail yard pushing over her quarterdeck, Captain Miller stepped forward to lead the boarders only to be stopped with the words, 'No Miller, I must have that honour.' Nelson later told Drinkwater that 'he knew the attempt was hazardous and his presence, he thought, might contribute to its success'.

Hazardous it certainly was. Paintings and prints of the action have tended to romanticize the scene, with an immaculately dressed commodore poised aesthetically at the head of his men. The reality was ugly, brutal and very far from poised (see illustration on p. 54). The *Captain's* cathead had become entangled with the stern gallery of the *San Nicolas*, creating a convenient bridge. A soldier from the 69th Regiment (onboard serving as marines) reached over and broke a stern window with his musket butt and Nelson then clambered out along the cathead and scrambled through the shattered glass into the Spanish captain's cabin, followed by his men. The cabin doors were locked and Spanish officers were firing their pistols through the windows; but the doors were broken open with axes and the boarders stormed on to the quarterdeck, cutting down the Spanish commodore, Don Tomas Geraldino, as they went. Meanwhile, another party, under Edward Berry, had run out along the bowsprit and dropped from the spritsail yard on to the quarterdeck. Moments later, Nelson was receiving the swords of the Spanish officers and a second Spanish ship was in British hands. According to the Spanish official returns, 127 of her crew had been killed or wounded – a casualty list of almost 25 per cent.

The even larger, three-decked *San José* was still trapped alongside the *San Nicolas*. The *Prince George* had her in her sights and was firing well-aimed broadsides into her, adding to the carnage created by the earlier broadsides from the *Captain* and *Excellent*. Rear Admiral Don Francisco Xavier Winthuysen had been carried below, having lost both legs earlier in the action, and over 150 of her crew – some 20 per cent – were already dead or wounded. Some of the survivors now started firing into Nelson's boarding party below them on the quarterdeck of the *San Nicolas*. It was an awkward moment: if the Spanish had managed to rally, Nelson and his small boarding party could easily have been overwhelmed.

'Westminster Abbey or glorious victory!'

As he led the boarders up the sides of the *San José* Nelson is supposed to have shouted, 'Westminster Abbey or glorious victory!' – which has given his famous exploit a rather theatrical air and made him appear slightly false and ridiculous. Certainly Nicolas thought so and dismissed the shout as 'a gasconade very inconsistent with his character'.

As so often with the more melodramatic utterances attributed to Nelson, the original source of the story is James Harrison's 1806 biography, (vol. I, p. 165) which was heavily influenced by Emma Hamilton. The section on the battle of Cape St Vincent – which Harrison acknowledges was drawn extensively from Drinkwater's *Narrative* – includes a reference to Nelson leading the new attack, 'vehemently exclaiming – "Westminster Abbey or glorious victory!"'.

By including the shout in the middle of a direct quotation from Drinkwater, Harrison implied that it was based on an original and contemporary source. However, the shout does not occur in Drinkwater's original 1797 edition and so, clearly, it was Harrison's own interpolation. For this reason it is suspect and my own view is that it was probably one of Emma's embellishments.

There now came the most extraordinary act in an extraordinary day. Summing up the situation rapidly, Nelson first placed sentries at the hatchways and hailed Miller, telling him to send reinforcements to keep the *San Nicolas* under control. Having thus secured his rear, he then led his boarding party in another furious rush – this time, up the sides of the *San José*, looming above them. Berry gave him a leg-up into her main chains, from where he leapt over the bulwark and down on to her quarterdeck. There, he was met by the Spanish captain, who presented his sword as a gesture of surrender, explaining that the admiral was dying of his wounds below.

Suspicious at this sudden collapse of resistance, Nelson asked the captain 'on his honour' if the ship had surrendered and, on being assured that she had, shook hands with him and told him to assemble his officers for a formal surrender ceremony:

. . . and on the quarterdeck of a Spanish first-rate, extravagant as the story may seem, did I receive the swords of the vanquished Spaniards; which as I received I

The surrender of the San José. *Daniel Orme's famous representation of the moment when Nelson received the surrender of his second prize is symbolic, rather than historically accurate. The Spanish admiral (lying left) was in fact dying below of his wounds and Nelson's own uniform was in tatters and his face smeared with gunsmoke.*

gave to William Fearney, one of my bargemen, who put them with the greatest sang-froid under his arm.

As he stood there, still dazed by what he and his men had achieved, one of his old *Agamemnon*s, Francis Cook, pushed up to him and shook him warmly by the hand, 'saying he might not soon have another place to do it in, and assured me he was heartily glad to see me'.

To have taken two ships in matter of minutes by clambering from one to the other was a quite remarkable – indeed, a unique – achievement. It captured the imagination of the victorious British fleet, who dubbed it 'Nelson's Patent Bridge for Boarding First Rates'; it has continued to inspire successive generations; it has been immortalized in numerous paintings – so much so, that it has become by far the most familiar image of the battle (see illustration on p. 67). Yet, that picture – of the hero receiving the Spanish swords by the armful – can give a distorted impression of how the contest was won. It must be remembered that the *San Nicolas* and *San José* had been battered by the combined broadsides of the *Captain*, *Culloden*, *Blenheim* and *Prince George* for almost two hours before being further assaulted by the *Excellent*. Without subtracting one jot from Nelson's personal gallantry, and that of his boarding party, it is possible to see that the British success in this, the decisive encounter of the battle, was due above all to the splendid teamwork of Jervis' well-trained force.

THE CLOSING STAGES

That teamwork was still operating, even as William Fearney was making up his bundle of swords 'with as much composure as he would tie a bundle of faggots', as Collingwood later put it. For looming amidst the Spanish fleet was the distinctive bulk of the *Santissima Trinidad*, now badly damaged by the concentrated broadsides she had endured for two hours. One after another, the British ships made their way towards her, inexorably drawn to such a tempting prize. Collingwood eventually reached her at about 1530; but by then his sails and rigging had been so badly shot about that he could not get close enough to hit her as hard as his previous victims. She was continuing to defend herself gallantly and the *Excellent* received more damage from her than from any previous opponent.

James Saumarez in the *Orion* was the next to win his laurels. After the *Salvador del Mundo* rehoisted her colours, she was engaged by both the *Victory* and the *Orion* and at about 1500 she eventually – and definitively – surrendered, having lost her captain, Antonio de Tepes and over 200 men killed and wounded, more than 25 per cent of her ship's company. This time, she was given no chance for second thoughts: Saumarez sent his first lieutenant across in a boat to take possession of her. He then moved on to join the group around the *Santissima Trinidad* at about 1600. The *Orion*'s heavy fire, combined with that of the *Excellent* and the *Blenheim*, sent her fore and mizzen masts over the side and killed or wounded more than 200 of her crew.

At that point, some of the British thought they saw first a white flag and then, when they did not cease firing, an English flag hoisted above a Spanish one. They were therefore convinced that the *Trinidad* had surrendered. But, at 1622, even as they prepared to take possession of their richest prize of all, the signal came from the *Victory* for the whole British fleet to wear and come on to the starboard tack, followed at 1639 by the order to form line ahead in close order. Jervis had decided to end the engagement, forcing the terriers gathered around the beleaguered Spanish flagship to relinquish their grip. Moments later, they saw their prize rehoist her colours and retire among her comrades.

Saumarez, who had been closest to her and the most hotly engaged, was certain he had seen the white flag. The logs of some of the other British ships bear him out. Córdoba, not unnaturally, makes no mention of this incident in his account of the battle; nor does the log of the *Blenheim*, the other British ship most closely engaged; and Collingwood, who was rather further off, later wrote, 'some say he struck – I did not see it'. However, modern research in the Spanish sources tends to support Saumarez's claim and so, on balance, it seems that the great ship almost certainly did surrender – but only moments before Jervis' signal.

Saumarez was bitterly disappointed to lose such a prestigious prize by such a narrow margin. He called Jervis' order 'ill-timed' and then added philosophically, 'but doubtless necessary'. Other commentators have been rather less generous and have accused Sir John of unnecessary caution. But, in judging his decision to end the action, it is important to see the whole picture that he had before him. The early sunset of a February day was fast approaching and he had four badly damaged prizes to secure, one of which, the *San Nicolas*, was on fire in her forehold. Many of his own ships had suffered serious damage – for example, the crew of the *Blenheim* later discovered that she had received 105 round shot in her hull alone and two of her foremost gunports had been battered into one. Three other British ships were in urgent need of assistance. The *Colossus*'s crew was still struggling to repair her earlier damage; having swayed up a topsail yard to replace the shattered foreyard, they were now setting a treble-reefed fore-topsail on it. At 1628, the *Captain* signalled that she needed boats to tow and the *Culloden*'s log records that she was leaking so much that she had to keep two chain pumps going all night – punishing labour for her men after the fatigues of the battle.

However, the deciding factor was that Jervis could see that the Spanish were beginning to rally. To the north, two Spanish ships (the *San Pablo* and *Pelayo* detached that morning) were now coming down to join their comrades. To the south, Moreno had finally worked his way round the British line and was now approaching with the convoy and four of his warships – a force which would have looked to the British like a further Spanish reinforcement of eight ships. In the circumstances, Jervis' decision to break off the action seems wholly justifiable.

As dusk fell, the two fleets drifted slowly apart, the British formed in a tight line of battle, protecting their own injured ships and their prizes. Both sides were counting their losses and making hasty repairs. During the last moments of the battle, Nelson had transferred his pendant to *La Minerve* which took him to the flagship for an encounter with his commander-in-chief. Any worries he may have had were soon dispelled for, the moment he appeared on the *Victory*'s quarterdeck, part of his hat shot away, his shirt and coat in tatters and his face still streaked with smoke, Jervis wrapped him in his arms and 'said he could not sufficiently thank me and used every expression to make me happy'. As Nelson

Nelson and the lessons of Cape St Vincent

Although it had many unorthodox features, Cape St Vincent was an old-fashioned battle in one important sense: Jervis remained in personal control throughout, manoeuvring his fleet by signals from the flagship. It would seem that Nelson recognized the problems that this centralization of command had caused – especially at the critical moment when the admiral's signals had not been seen by the *Britannia*.

When his turn came to command a fleet in battle, Nelson dealt with the problem of control in two key ways. First, he made a close study of signalling and kept up to date with any developments that would make it easier for him to make his intentions clear. For example, shortly before leaving for Trafalgar he made arrangements for copies of Sir Home Popham's new signal code – then 'hot off the press' – to be sent out to his fleet. It was of course this code that enabled him to send his famous message, 'England Expects' – which would have been impossible with any previous system.

Second, Nelson made sure that all his captains knew his intentions thoroughly beforehand – by giving them what we would now call 'briefings' – and he stressed the importance of personal initiative. For example, in a memorandum setting out his tactical plans in 1803, he said he was,

> fully assured that the admirals and captains of the fleet I have the honour to command will, knowing my precise object, that of a close and decisive battle, supply any deficiency of my not making signals, which may, if extended beyond these objects, either be misunderstood, or if waited for very probably from various causes be impossible for the commander-in-chief to make. (J.S. Corbett, *Fighting Instructions*, NRS, vol. 29)

In that passage, we can catch an echo of the mounting frustration he must have felt at Cape St Vincent as, with one eye on the approaching Spaniards, he waited in vain for the *Britannia* to obey Jervis' signal and change course.

was rowed away, cheers ringing in his ears, to hoist his pendant in the comparatively undamaged *Irresistible*, Calder, out of step to the last, commented disparagingly that Nelson's remarkable initiative had been contrary to orders. 'It certainly was so,' replied Jervis, 'and if you ever commit such a breach of orders I will forgive you also.'

Córdoba, too, was on the move. Once the battle was over, he transferred with his staff to the frigate *Diana*, the better to supervise operations during the night. As the reports began to come in, the scale of the defeat became increasingly apparent. Besides the four ships lost to the British, the *Trinidad* was a dismasted hulk and three other battleships, the *Concepcion*, *Mexicano* and *Soberano* were so badly damaged that they were unable to renew the action. His official dispatch, written before all the returns were in, mentioned some 600 killed and wounded but the later, official figures were 200 killed and 1,284 wounded. The official British figures were disproportionately small: 73 killed and 227 wounded.

The following day, 15 February, the British continued repairing their battle damage, while watching closely for an attack which they felt sure must come from the reinforced Spanish fleet, still in sight to the north-west. As the morning wore on, there appeared to be no movement but then, at about 1100, they were seen to be advancing. The signal was made to close around the *Victory* and then to form line of battle. This show of strength convinced Córdoba that further action was impractical and so he now concentrated his efforts in getting his fleet and convoy into Cádiz. As the Spanish withdrew, the British ships hoisted Spanish colours as a mark of respect for the unfortunate Winthuysen, who had died in the night. They then made their way to the shelter of Lagos Bay to complete their repairs.

The sword of Admiral Winthuysen in the Guildhall at Norwich. Nelson presented the sword to the city and this special trophy was designed to house it.

TRAFALGAR

The Sword of the Spanish Admiral.
DON XAVIER WINTHUYSEN:
who died of the Wounds he received in that Engagement with the British Fleet, under the command of Admiral EARL S.t VINCENT, 14.th Feb.y 1797: which ended in the most brilliant Victory ever obtain'd by this Country over the Enemy at Sea: wherein the heroic Valour and cool determined Courage, of Rear Admiral S.r HORATIO NELSON, K.B. had ample scope for their display. He being a native of Norfolk, honour'd the City by Presenting this Sword surrender'd to him in that Action.

PALMAM · QUI · MERUIT · FERAT ·

CHAPTER SIX

'The most glorious Valentine's Day'
Celebrating the battle

'I rejoice you have at last begun to be noticed in a proper manner.'
Fanny Nelson to her husband, 3 April 1797

JERVIS' DISPATCH

As the victorious British ships gathered in Lagos Bay, Nelson found that he was, as he told Fanny, 'rich in the praise of every man from the highest to the lowest in this fleet'. His exploit in capturing the *San José* from the deck of the *San Nicolas* was dubbed, 'Nelson's Patent Bridge for Boarding First Rates', and a spoof recipe was circulated, 'Commodore Nelson's receipt for making an Olla Podrida'. This involved 'battering and basting' a Spanish first rate and 80-gun ship to prepare a dish, 'fit to set before His Majesty'.

On the morning after the battle, he received warm letters of congratulation, including one from his old friend Collingwood, 'The highest rewards are due to you and the *Culloden*; you formed the plan of attack – we were only accessories to the Dons' ruin.' And another from Sir Gilbert Elliot,

> You will easily believe, I trust, the joy with which I witnessed your glory yesterday. To have had any share in it is an honour enough for one man's life, but to have been foremost on such a day could fall to your share alone.

Some days later, still basking in this praise, Nelson wrote to his uncle, William Suckling, 'all do me the justice I deserve'. At this point he was obviously convinced that his long wait for public recognition was at an end and that, when

Sir John Jervis' official dispatch was published, the name of Nelson would be prominently featured. He was about to be severely disappointed.

'Although I do not much profess to like fighting,' Jervis had written to a friend, 'I would much rather have an action with the enemy than detail one.' Like everyone else in the Navy, he had deplored the dispatch Admiral Lord Howe had written after the Glorious First of June in 1794, which had singled out some captains for special praise and omitted to mention others equally deserving. So determined was Jervis to avoid the same mistake that he erred in the opposite direction, producing a dispatch that was short to the point of terseness. It made no mention at all of individuals except for Captain Calder, 'whose able assistance has greatly contributed to the public service during my command'. Bearing in mind the complete lack of sympathy between the two men during the battle, one suspects that Jervis was doing his best to rid himself of an unwanted subordinate.

When this dispatch was published, it caused outrage among Nelson's friends and the rumour even began circulating that Jervis had originally intended to mention the commodore and his exploits, but had been persuaded against it by a jealous Calder. In view of Jervis' low opinion of his flag captain, it is unlikely that he would have been influenced by him in such an important matter and, in any case, we now know that he had explained the reasons for his reticence in a private letter to the First Lord which accompanied the dispatch,

> The correct conduct of every Officer and man in the Squadron on the 14th inst made it improper to distinguish one more than another in my public Letter, because I am confident that had those who were least in action been in the situation of the fortunate few, their behaviour would not have been less meritorious.

He then went on to highlight those whom he felt had distinguished themselves most, mentioning specifically, Troubridge, Collingwood – and Nelson, 'who contributed very much to the fortune of the day'.

In fairness to Jervis, when he said that it was 'improper to distinguish one more than another', it is clear that he was reflecting the opinions of a number of his subordinates. Collingwood, one of those who had suffered as a result of Howe's unfair singling out of individuals, wrote to his uncle by marriage,

> What is particularly happy about this great event is that there is no drawback, no slander – though not all were equally engaged . . . I understand the Admiral has wisely avoided all partial praise of particular acts, which might insinuate to the disadvantage of all those whose ill-luck prevented their getting into conspicuous situations.

And Ralph Miller wrote to his father,

> I will only say that among the pleasant things of this glorious day one considerable one is there being no drawback, nobody against whom there is a breath of Censure – every ship was at one part of the day engag'd but situation did not admit of all being equally so.

The striking similarity in the wording of these two comments suggests that they reflect fairly accurately the table-talk and gossip of the fleet.

Nelson made no mention in any of his letters at this time of his disappointment at Jervis' failure to make his exploits public; but a tell-tale remark in a letter written much later, in 1803, shows that he was deeply hurt. Replying to a letter from Admiral Waldegrave in which the older man had mentioned their joint exploits at Cape St Vincent, he wrote: 'I owe much of my fame on that day to your truly honourable mind; but for you it would hardly have [been] known I was present.'

We do not know exactly what Waldegrave had done to deserve Nelson's gratitude – but he certainly was not alone in publicizing the commodore's exploits. Two other key players in the creation of the Nelson Legend were Sir Gilbert Elliot and his aide, Colonel John Drinkwater. Having watched the battle from the quarterdeck of HMS *Lively*, the viceroy and his staff sailed in her for England on 19 February, accompanied by Calder who was carrying home Jervis' dispatch. They were delayed by an easterly wind in the Channel and Calder became anxious that someone else might arrive first with the news and rob him of his moment of glory. So he gave orders for the frigate to put into St Ives in Cornwall, where he went ashore insisting, according to Drinkwater, 'that no letters, nor any other person than himself and servant should be allowed to land'.

The *Lively* eventually reached Plymouth on 5 March, where they found the French and Spanish fleets were expected in the Channel at any moment. The Bank of England had just suspended payments and the whole country was in a state of alarm so, in such circumstances, the news of the victory at Cape St Vincent caused a huge wave of relief. Elliot and Drinkwater drove to London where they found celebrations already under way: Calder had arrived a few days earlier and Jervis' dispatch had been published in a special edition of the *London Gazette* on 3 March. When it was known that they had been present at the battle, they were pressed for a more detailed account of what had happened and it was then that they discovered how meagre the admiral's dispatch had been. Even more surprising was the omission of Nelson's name from the accounts that were circulating. As Drinkwater later remembered,

> The whole of the British Squadron had not hesitated to bestow on him the chief merit of the enemy's defeat; therefore not to have his name mentioned in the

public despatch . . . produced no small degree of surprise among the Commodore's friends.

Drinkwater had already sketched some diagrams of the battle which he had intended to publish and he now decided to accompany them with a description of the fighting. But this was not to be a broad-brush narrative from the standpoint of a distant onlooker, for the colonel had received a detailed account of the most dramatic events from the man most closely involved – Commodore Nelson himself.

NELSON TELLS HIS STORY

On the morning of 15 February, while the British continued repairing their battle damage and burying their dead, there had also been time for courtesy calls and letters of congratulation. Collingwood received a warm letter from Waldegrave saying that, 'nothing in my opinion could exceed the spirit and true officership which you so happily displayed yesterday'; while Sir Gilbert Elliot and Lord Garlies, captain of HMS *Lively*, were rowed across to the *Victory* to call on Sir John Jervis.

The boat was small and there was no room for Drinkwater. As he stood on the quarterdeck watching the viceroy's departure, he noticed another boat approaching from a different direction and, when it came closer, saw that Nelson was on board. Moments later, the commodore was at his side asking eagerly for Sir Gilbert. When Drinkwater explained that he had just left, Nelson was clearly disappointed. 'I had hoped to have caught him before he saw the Admiral,' he said, 'but come below with me', and led the way to Captain Lord Garlies' cabin.

A remarkable conversation ensued and Drinkwater made pencil notes on a scrap of paper he found close to hand. A rather formal and stately man himself, his account of their talk shows he obviously felt he was taking a liberty in interrogating the hero of the hour so closely: 'In the animation of the conversation, I went so far as to ask, "How came you Commodore, to get into that singular and perilous situation?"' he recalled ponderously. But he had mistaken his man. Nelson had no objection at all to talking about himself: 'I'll tell you,' he replied good-naturedly and then plunged into a detailed account, first of his decision to join the van and then, 'with increased animation', of his boarding exploits.

Nelson's opening question to Drinkwater on the *Lively*'s quarterdeck gave the game away: he had obviously come with the express purpose of telling his story. He knew that Elliot would be returning immediately to England to bring the latest news of the situation in Italy to his superiors in London and had guessed that the *Lively* would carry the first news of the battle, including the admiral's official dispatch. So he was anxious to make sure that his influential friend the viceroy had full particulars of his dashing exploits. And if the top man was not available, he was content to make do with the aide-de-camp.

Drinkwater did not let him down. Although in his *Narrative*, he was careful to emphasize that, 'the whole squadron has gained immortal honour', inevitably this attempt at even-handedness went almost unnoticed. Nelson's actions had a glamour about them that was instantly appealing and they were more easy for laymen to understand than the important, but less dramatic, contributions of Collingwood or Saumarez. So Nelson's story hit the headlines and the exploits of his fellow officers were largely overlooked.

In any case, by the time Drinkwater's *Narrative* was published, an even more detailed account of Nelson's actions had already appeared in the *Sun* on 20 March – and, this time, the author was Nelson himself. Shortly after the battle, he had produced his own unofficial report, *A few remarks relative to myself in the* Captain, *in which my pendant was flying on the most glorious Valentine's Day, 1797*, which he then sent to a number of key people – including Waldegrave (who was about to return to England), his friend the Duke of Clarence (third son of King George III) and his old mentor, Captain William Locker. To Locker he said,

> if you approve of it, [you] are at perfect liberty to insert it in the newspapers, inserting the name of Commodore instead of 'I' . . . As I do not write for the press there may be some parts of it which require the pruning knife, which I desire you to do without fear.

Locker duly obliged and it was thanks to him that the account was published by the *Sun*. But he did not follow Nelson's request to use the 'pruning knife'. Instead it was printed with all the 'I's intact, as his pupil's personal account.

Despite their rather vainglorious tone, the *Remarks* did much to enhance Nelson's reputation in influential circles. Fanny passed a copy to his former patron, Admiral Lord Hood, who told her that her husband's deeds would 'immortalise his name in the pages of English history' and added that he had taken the opportunity to show it 'where he knew it would be of service'. She also reported that the Duke of Clarence had been 'loud in his praise' at a recent Court function.

Nelson also sent a copy of the *Remarks* to the Mayor of Norwich, together with the sword of Admiral Winthuysen, explaining,

> being born in the County of Norfolk, I beg leave to present the Sword to the City of Norwich, in order to its being preserved as a Memento of the Event, and of my Affection for my Native County.

The St Vincent controversy

Nelson's *Remarks* were not universally well received, for they contained a passage which offended some of his colleagues in the fleet.

As we have seen (p. 56), when the *Captain* crossed over to join the van, she took her place at the head of the British line, just in front of the *Culloden*. The wind was blowing their gunsmoke astern of them and so Nelson and Miller apparently did not see that the *Blenheim* and the rest of the van were close behind the *Culloden*, and joined the action at almost exactly the same time. In his letter to his father, Miller wrote, 'The *Culloden* and ourselves remained a full hour the only ships engaged with this body' and Nelson echoed this phrase in the *Remarks*, 'For an hour the *Culloden* and the *Captain* supported this apparently, but not in reality, unequal contest.'

This claim was resented: when the *Remarks* appeared in the *Sun*, Rear Admiral William Parker, who had commanded the van, challenged Nelson's statement in a long letter, which he then arranged to have published. Parker's style is extraordinarily turgid and difficult to follow but one phrase does stand out, 'therefore, so different to your statement, very soon after you commenced your fire, you had four ships pressing on board of each other, close in your rear'. (*Naval Chronicle*, XXI, pp. 302–4.) In response to this protest, Nelson altered his account, rather grudgingly, to 'for near an hour as I believe (but do not pretend to be correct as to time)'.

It was an unedifying spat that took a little of the shine off the glory of the victory – but is only fair to Parker to add that close examination of the logbooks of all the ships involved has established that he and his colleagues were right and so it is their version of events that is now accepted, rather than Nelson's.

In response, he was made an Honorary Freeman of Norwich and the sword was placed in a special case in the Guildhall, where it remains to this day (see illustration on p. 72). But the gesture caused some local jealousy: Nelson's eldest brother Maurice, who worked as a clerk at the Navy Office, later told Fanny Nelson that King's Lynn (which was, after all, closer to Burnham Thorpe than Norwich) 'wish that the sword had been given to them'.

So it was that, despite Jervis' reticence, when the news of Cape St Vincent was celebrated with the customary bells, bonfires and popular celebrations, Nelson's

Commemorative snuff box. The rhyme on the lid attributes the capture of the
Salvador del Mundo *to Nelson: in fact she was captured by Captain James Saumarez.*

name featured prominently. From Bath, Nelson's father wrote in his quaint manner,

> The name and services of Nelson have sounded throughout the city of Bath,
> from the common ballad-singer to the public theatre. Joy sparkles in every eye,
> and desponding Britain draws back the sable veil and smiles.

The victory produced a flood of commemorative material – much of which
highlighted Nelson. *The Times* published the recipe for 'Olla Podrida' which had
been circulating in the fleet. Most of the prints of the battle depicted the *Captain*
in action – some of them actually based on sketches produced by Miller. Even the
popular souvenirs tended to concentrate on Nelson's deeds: a crude *papier mâché*
box (above) bore the slogan,

> To Nelson fill bumbo
> For taking del Mundo

The *Salvador del Mundo* had of course been captured by the joint efforts of Collingwood
and Saumarez – but one searches in vain for similar items commemorating their deeds.

The echoes of this adulation eventually reached Nelson off Cádiz on 1 April, when he received forty letters of congratulation, together with all the newspapers. Fanny Nelson wrote three letters in a fortnight, each one filled with messages of congratulation from family and friends – although she could not resist adding a plaintive plea, 'You have done desperate actions enough. Now may I, indeed I do beg, that you never board again. *Leave* it for *Captains*.' Some friends wrote directly, among them, Lord Hood, the Duke of Clarence – and Margaret Parker, wife of his patron, Sir Peter Parker, who said,

> your conduct on the memorable 14th of February, a proud day for Old England, is above all praise; it never was nor ever can be equalled. All that I shall say is, your mother could not have heard of your deeds with more affection, nor could she be more rejoiced at your personal escape from all the dangers to which you were exposed on that glorious day.

'Leave it for Captains'

Nelson's biographers have tended to be critical of Fanny Nelson for her timorous response to her husband's daring actions at Cape St Vincent. Even Carola Oman places her plea immediately after an extract from Lady Parker's more robust letter and calls it 'the still small voice of Virgilia' after 'the trumpet call of Volumnia' (Oman, p. 216).

Fanny, like Nelson himself, has suffered from selective quotation and, in this case, the offender was Nicolas. He was the first to print her letter (vol. II, p. 359), but he edited it heavily – the very offence for which he so berated Clarke and M'Arthur. The full text, published by Naish (pp. 350–2), reveals that Fanny's request to 'Leave it for Captains' came towards the end of a long letter in which she told Nelson proudly of all the kind things that people had said about him and passed on the congratulations of a number of their family and friends. Most of these other, more positive, references are omitted in Nicolas's extract.

Nicolas then made matters worse by adding an even shorter extract from Fanny's next letter of 20 March, which further enforced the impression of her timidity and which has also been much quoted by Nelson's biographers. But, once again, the passage came in the middle of a long list of eulogies – and in this case, Nicolas omitted them all. (For the full letter, see Naish, pp. 352–5).

Certainly, Fanny was no heroine and could not prevent her natural anxiety breaking out. But a fair reading of the complete letters shows that she was trying her best to please her extraordinary husband.

Frances, Lady Nelson. This watercolour, painted after Nelson's death, captures Fanny's quiet, genteel beauty and, above all, her unswerving devotion to her husband. In front of the bust on the table is a casket containing the miniature of him painted in Leghorn in 1794 (see p. 4) which she always kept with her.

MEMENTOES OF THE BATTLE

From that last phrase, it appears that it was not generally known that Nelson had been wounded. In his *Remarks* he dismissed his 'bruises' as 'trifling' but shortly after the battle they began to trouble him. Modern medical research has traced the development of his symptoms from passing references to them in his letters. First he suffered an inflammation in his bowels where he had been struck; then, a few days later, there was a stoppage of urine, probably caused by a blood clot in his uretha. Although these immediate problems wore off fairly quickly, they left an abdominal weakness, or hernia, which remained with him for the rest of his life. Although normally dormant, it was exacerbated by coughing, when it would form a lump in his side the size of a man's fist, causing him considerable pain.

He had another more pleasant memento, news of which also reached him on 1 April. The government marked the victory with lavish rewards. Jervis, who had already been created a baron a few weeks before the battle for his services in the Mediterranean, made a direct leap to earl, with a pension of £3,000 a year. Admirals Thompson and Parker were made baronets. Waldegrave, as the son of a peer, was already senior to a baronet, so eventually he was given an Irish peerage as Lord Radstock. All the flag-officers and captains received a gold medal, similar in design to one first instituted to commemorate the Battle of the Glorious First of June in 1794.

Nelson, as a junior flag-officer, was entitled to a baronetcy; but he wanted the Order of the Bath, with its distinctive star and ribbon, and wrote to Sir Gilbert Elliot asking him to intercede for him. He also mentioned his preference to Drinkwater during their conversation in the *Lively*'s cabin, 'As for you Commodore,' said Drinkwater, 'they will make you a Baronet.'

> The word was scarcely uttered, when placing his hand on my arm, and looking me most expressively in the face, he said, 'No, no: if they want to mark my services, it must not be in that manner.' 'Oh,' said I, interrupting him, 'you wish to be made a Knight of Bath.' . . . 'Yes, if my services have been of any value let them be noticed in a way that the public may know me.'

Once again, Drinkwater gives us a vivid glimpse of Nelson as his contemporaries saw and heard him.

Elliot duly intervened and, as there was a vacancy at that time, Nelson did indeed become a Knight of the Bath, with the right to wear a star on the left breast of his uniform coat. His long-awaited promotion had also come through at last and so he was now Rear Admiral Sir Horatio Nelson, KB. Lord Spencer's letter telling him of the knighthood said that it was being made,

> . . . in order to mark His Majesty's approbation of your successful and gallant exertions on several occasions during the course of the present war in the

Nelson's coat of arms. The first, and simplest, version of Nelson's coat of arms contains a number of allusions to Cape St Vincent. The lion is tearing a Spanish flag; the sailor is holding a staff with a commodore's pendant attached to it and the crest, above the helmet, is the stern of the San José.

Mediterranean, and more particularly of your very distinguished conduct in the glorious and brilliant Victory obtained over the Fleet of Spain.

The handsome reference to his 'successful and gallant exertions' pleased Nelson. 'It is well when we seem to satisfy all the world,' he wrote to Fanny, telling her in confidence about his knighthood. '. . . My chains and medals and ribbons, with a contented mind, are all sufficient' and, in the months that followed, he amused himself by designing his coat of arms with its supporters and motto. He included a number of references to Cape St Vincent: for example, his crest was the stern of the *San José* and it later appeared as the identifying mark on all his personal silver.

The presentation of the ring

The story of the presentation of the sword and ring has been known since 1845, when Nicolas was told it by Miller's sister, Mrs Dalrymple. He included it as a footnote on p. 342 of volume II of his *Dispatches*, where the implication was made (often followed by Nelson's biographers) that the event occurred on the evening of the battle.

However, in the recently discovered letter to his father, written on 3 March 1797 (see Appendix 1, pp. 155–9), Miller says quite clearly that Nelson visited the *Captain* on the morning of 15 February.

Nelson's apparent obsession with promoting his own public image can appear unattractive and so it is only fair to emphasize once more that he had been unfairly treated in the past. In the circumstances, it is hardly surprising that he made the most of his remarkable exploits at Cape St Vincent and did all he could to make the public aware of them.

Moreover, his apparent self-centredness was always balanced by a willingness to acknowledge the part that others had played in helping him win glory. We have seen already how, in his dispatch after the capture of the *Santa Sabina*, he went out of his way to praise Captain Cockburn and the other officers – and the same pattern of behaviour can be seen after Cape St Vincent.

At about the time he called on Drinkwater in the *Lively*, he also paid a visit to his shattered pendant ship, HMS *Captain*, where Ralph Miller and his crew were busy repairing the extensive battle damage. Taking Miller into the cabin, he exclaimed, 'Miller, I am under the greatest obligations to you' and presented him with one of the Spanish swords which his coxswain had bundled up under his arm the previous afternoon. Then, apparently feeling that something more was needed, he drew a ring from his own finger, 'a Topaz set round in diamonds', and placed it on Miller's finger as a token of his esteem. 'And indeed,' wrote Miller to his father, 'I feel satisfied that our friendship will last as long as ourselves – those four glorious hours became more than years in affection.'

Nelson was very good at nurturing friendships. Earlier that morning, he had found time to write to Collingwood:

My dearest friend, 'A friend in need is a friend indeed', was never more truly verified than by your most noble and gallant conduct yesterday in sparing the *Captain* from further loss; and I beg, both as a public Officer and a friend, you will accept my most sincere thanks. I have not failed, by letter to the Admiral, to represent the eminent services of the *Excellent*.

A few days later he wrote to William Hoste's father, the Revd Dixon Hoste,

You will be anxious to hear a line of your good and brave William after the sharp services of the *Captain* on the 14th. I have hitherto said so much of my dear William, that I can only repeat his gallantry never can be exceeded, and that each day rivets him stronger to my heart.

Scarcely surprising, then, that his officers adored him. Young Hoste later spoke of 'him whom, I may say, has been a second father to me' and when Maurice Nelson met two of his brother's young lieutenants, he told Fanny, 'They both speak in raptures and look upon my brother as their father.'

SOURCES FOR PART TWO

The signals and extracts from log entries used in the battle narrative have all been taken from T. Sturges Jackson (ed.), *The Logs of the Great Sea Fights*, Vol. I. As usual, the timings in the different logs differ widely and so, wherever possible, I have 'corrected' times to agree with the *Victory*'s time. So, for example, the *Captain*'s times are consistently 10–15 minutes ahead of the *Victory*'s and it is important to take account of this when assessing Nelson's actions.

Our current understanding of the battle, especially the new appreciation of the importance of Jervis' role, has been very largely due to the work of two historians. In 1954, in both the *Mariner's Mirror* and *The Naval Review*, A.H. Taylor was the first to draw attention to the presence of the Spanish convoy and also to tell the story of the battle from Jervis' point of view. In 1991, in the *Mariner's Mirror*, M.A.J. Palmer's masterly analysis of the signals and log entries greatly increased our understanding of the opening stages of the battle and of Jervis' tactical intentions. In 1997, I continued Palmer's research processes to include the rest of the battle and the preceding reconnaissance in my monograph, *The Battle of Cape St Vincent*.

The new insights about Jervis' character come from my colleague Clive Wilkinson, whose new biography, based on the research he carried out with the late Professor Emilio Moriconi, is eagerly awaited. In the meantime, an idea of their joint thesis can be gained from Clive Wilkinson's paper, 'Sir John Jervis: The Man for the Occasion' published in the *St Vincent 200* conference proceedings.

Miller's letter to his father describing his part in the battle is a new discovery, which I found among the papers in the Nelson Collection at Lloyds in 1997 during research for the Royal Naval Museum's Nelson Biography Project. It is printed in full, with explanatory notes, at Appendix 1.

All the other personal correspondence quoted comes from printed sources, details of which will be found in the Bibliography.

For the medical analysis of Nelson's Cape St Vincent wound, I am indebted to Dr Anne-Marie Hills, who kindly allowed me to study her extensive and illuminating research on Nelson's health. For a fuller discussion of the wound and Nelson's subsequent symptoms see her article, 'His Belly at Cape St Vincent' in the *St Vincent 200* conference proceedings.

For British readers, the main new insights in this section will be those relating to the difficulties under which the Spanish fleet was labouring and its signals and manoeuvres during the battle. All of these are drawn from the latest researches of Spanish naval historians. For a brief resumé of these new findings, see Hugo O'Donnell's *St Vincent 200* paper: 'The Spanish Navy in the 18th Century'.

A translation of Córdoba's dispatch was published, in a somewhat garbled form, as an appendix in J. Ross, *Memoirs and Correspondence of Admiral Lord de Saumarez*.

The first edition of Drinkwater's *Narrative*, published in 1797, is a straightforward account of the Battle of Cape St Vincent, with a most useful set of diagrams. However, in 1840, Drinkwater reissued his book to raise funds for the proposed Nelson monument, and took the opportunity to expand the Nelsonian material. It is from this second edition that the stories about the voyage of *La Minerve* and Nelson's visit to the *Lively* on the morning after the battle are taken.

PART THREE

The attack on Santa Cruz de Tenerife, July 1797

The boat action off Cádiz, 4 July 1797. This pen and wash drawing by William Bromley captures vividly the ferocity and confusion of Nelson's bloody little action with the Spanish gun-boats.

CHAPTER SEVEN

'Parading under the walls of Cádiz'

The British blockade

'The Dons are all in port and I believe it will be a very difficult matter
to get them out again.'
Nelson to his wife, 12 April 1797

BOMBARDING CÁDIZ

In the small hours of 4 July 1797, the British bombarded Cádiz. Having trailed their coats outside the port for almost three months, daring the Spanish fleet to emerge and fight another battle, they were now attempting to force them out. A Dutch galliot had been fitted with a mortar and a howitzer in Gibraltar, renamed the *Thunder*, and sent to join Sir John Jervis' fleet under the command of Lieutenant John Gowerley. On board was Lieutenant Baines of the Royal Artillery, who was to supervise a bombardment of the town and naval dockyard.

The position from which the *Thunder* was to make her attack had been carefully pinpointed the previous afternoon by Lieutenant Baines, accompanied by Ralph Miller, who had commanded the *Captain* at Cape St Vincent. Miller was well known as a particularly active and ingenious officer and now he had been placed in charge of the tricky operation of manoeuvring the unwieldy vessel to the correct spot. But, despite all his efforts, the operation did not go entirely smoothly: when he went in his boat to guide the bomb-vessel in, he found her steering six points wide of her course and, even after it had been agreed that he would go ahead of her and show her the way, further orders were shouted from her that caused considerable confusion. To his surprise he found that Rear Admiral Sir Horatio Nelson was on board, commanding the operation in person – and, for all his admiration for the admiral, Miller was becoming impatient at Nelson's tendency to interfere with the minutiae of operational matters.

Miller died young, at the Siege of Acre in 1799, before a formal portrait could be painted of him. This is the only known likeness of him, made for special prints commemorating the Battles of Cape St Vincent (see p. 28) and the Nile.

Captain Ralph Miller

This description of the bombardment of Cádiz contains rather more detail than has hitherto been available to historians because of the recent discovery of a private account of the Cádiz and Tenerife operations written for his wife by Captain Ralph Miller (see 'Sources' section, p. 146).

Miller was undoubtedly one of the bright stars of Jervis' fleet: 'an officer of the first merit', as his obituary in the *Naval Chronicle* put it. Having been educated at the Naval Academy in Portsmouth, he first went to sea in 1778 and saw much service in the American war, including a number of fleet actions. In 1793, he took part in the operations at Toulon and afterwards in the capture of Corsica, where he first met Nelson.

When Nelson moved to HMS *Captain* as commodore in June 1796, he asked for Miller as his captain. After Cape St Vincent, the two men moved to the *Theseus* and continued to serve together until Nelson left the fleet to recover from the loss of his arm in August 1797. Miller remained in the *Theseus* and commanded her at the Battle of the Nile in August 1798 and the Siege of Acre in 1799, where he was killed by a bursting shell on 14 May.

Miller left a number of accounts of the actions in which he was involved. His very detailed record of the Nile was published by Nicolas in the addenda to his volume VII but the other two are both very recent discoveries: Cape St Vincent (uncovered in 1997 and published by The 1805 Club – and printed again here as Appendix 1) and Cádiz and Tenerife (to be published by The 1805 Club). They are not only vivid and detailed but also extremely frank – so they are invaluable cross-references to the official, and often rather sanitized, accounts.

The *Thunder* finally found her position and began bombarding. But it was a clear, moonlit night and the delay had given the Spanish time to see what was happening. So, within moments, a flotilla of gun and mortar boats was seen heading for the bomb-vessel. The British had expected such a counter-attack, so the *Thunder* had been escorted by all the available boats in the British fleet and Nelson now ordered Miller to take a detachment and head off the Spanish. Miller began to gather his forces, but he quickly found that very few of them were prepared to leave the reassuring shelter of the bomb-vessel. With every moment, the Spanish attack was becoming increasingly threatening and there was a real danger that the *Thunder* would be overwhelmed.

Suddenly, Miller heard a cry of 'Follow the admiral!' and a small boat shot away from the bomb-vessel's side. Seeing the problem, Nelson had leapt into his own barge and was leading the counter-attack himself. Redoubling their efforts, Miller's crew caught up with the admiral and together the two boats smashed into the head of the approaching flotilla. It was like the Battle of Cape St Vincent in miniature. Miller's boat rammed into the side of a Spanish mortar boat which had turned away and was trying to escape. While the men in the stern boomed the British off with their oars and fired into them with pistols and a swivel gun, the men in the bow went on rowing furiously. The British had dropped their oars, ready to board, and so the mortar boat was able to pull away. As Miller and his men struggled to get hold of their oars again to begin pursuing, they drifted down on to the starboard side of a much larger Spanish boat and, looking across, Miller spotted that it was already engaged with Nelson's barge.

Nelson's craft was much smaller than his opponent's and he had with him only a crew of ten and Captain Thomas Fremantle, who had joined the fleet off Cádiz that afternoon. The Spanish boat had thirty men on board, including the commander of the whole flotilla, Don Miguel Tyrason. So, by the time Miller arrived, Nelson and his men were in serious difficulty. Nelson himself had nearly been killed twice but, each time, his coxswain John Sykes had saved him: as one of Sykes's comrades later remembered, 'he seemed more concerned with the Admiral's life than with his own: he hardly ever struck a blow but to save his gallant officer'.

But then came a blow that even Sykes could not parry: a deadly descending sweep of a sabre or cutlass that could easily have severed Nelson's head. Reaching up, the sailor put his own hand in the path of the blow. 'We all saw it . . . and we gave in revenge one cheer and one tremendous rally'. At about the same moment, Miller's men boarded the Spanish boat from the other side and, after a brave resistance, in which eighteen men were killed, her crew surrendered and Don Miguel was taken prisoner.

In the meantime, the rest of the British boats had got into action and the Spanish flotilla turned and retreated into Cádiz. Miller pursued them, leaving Nelson cradling his wounded coxswain in his arms, 'Sykes,' he was heard to say, 'I cannot forget this', and he was as good as his word. He mentioned him by name in his official dispatch – at that time, a most unusual honour for a rating – and endeavoured to get him made a lieutenant. But Sykes had not served sufficient time as a petty officer to qualify for promotion and so he had to be satisfied with a gunner's warrant. Unfortunately, he died in October 1799 before he could reach commissioned rank.

Nelson also remembered Sykes when he recalled the incident in the autobiographical 'Sketch of my Life' which he prepared in October 1799. He was obviously very proud of his exploits off Cádiz. 'It was at this period,' he wrote, 'that perhaps my personal courage was more conspicuous than at any other period in my life.' Certainly, the bloody little action with the Spanish gun-boat, coming so soon after the 'Patent Bridge for Boarding First Rates', confirmed Nelson's reputation for personal bravery. Jervis said in his official report that he was 'always present in the most arduous enterprises' and, in a private letter to Nelson was even more effusive: 'Every service you are engaged in adds fresh lustre to the British arms and to your character.' It is clear, too, that Nelson's insistence on sharing danger with his junior officers and men did much to bind them to him:

'My personal courage'

'It was during this period that perhaps my personal courage was more conspicuous than at any other period in my life.' Perhaps more than anything else that he said or wrote, this sentence has reinforced Nelson's reputation for unattractive vanity. It is therefore only fair to point out that he did not expect that these words would be published.

The sentence occurs in some notes – he called them a 'Sketch' – which he jotted down in October 1799 at the request of John M'Arthur, who was preparing a biographical article for publication in the *Naval Chronicle*, of which he was the editor. In his covering letter, Nelson said that his 'Sketch', 'wants the pruning knife before it is fit to meet the public eye therefore I trust you and your friend will do that and turn it into much better language'. M'Arthur duly obliged and, when the biography was published in the *Chronicle* (vol. III, pp. 170–85) the passage had been altered to the unexceptionable statement, 'During this service, his personal courage, if possible, was more conspicuous than at any other period of his former service.'

However, M'Arthur kept the 'Sketch' and when, in 1809, he and his colleague the Revd James Stanier Clarke published their two-volume *Life*, they decided to print it in full, thus creating the impression that Nelson had intended to address posterity in this direct, and unattractively self-congratulatory manner.

'Rear Admiral Nelson's conflict in his barge with a Spanish launch.' This very stylized picture by Richard Westall was prepared for Clarke and M'Arthur's semi-official biography in 1809. Comparison with Bromley's realistic version of the same incident (see p. 88) highlights how Westall deliberately treated the event in a more 'heroic' style.

time and again in their memoirs or letters home it is his gallantry that is singled out for praise.

All the same, it should not have been necessary for the admiral to expose himself to such danger and, indeed, some of Nelson's biographers have questioned whether he should have taken part in the boat action at all. In his official dispatch Nelson gave no explanation of his actions, saying only, 'I directed a vigorous attack to be made on them, which was done with such gallantry, that they were drove and pursued close to the walls of Cádiz.' Ralph Miller's newly discovered account provides the explanation which Nelson was too tactful to reveal: the British boats were hesitating and he obviously decided that the only way to get them to move fast enough was to lead the counter-attack himself. Once again, he had demonstrated his ability to sense the decisive moment in a battle and his instinct for leading by personal example.

Nelson at this time was clearly a happy man. He had won the public recognition he craved and the admiration of his colleagues. He had achieved flag rank at last and was enjoying his new responsibilities as an admiral. After a long period of detached duty, he was now surrounded by friends in the fleet, with whom he was dining regularly and exchanging ideas for new operations. And, above all, he was working closely with his revered commander-in-chief, who constantly spoke of the 'utmost confidence' he reposed in his gifted subordinate. Jervis had a number of senior flag-officers with him in his fleet but he was out of sympathy with them all and so, in the absence of a second in command he could trust, it was always Nelson who was selected for special duties.

THE BLOCKADE OF CÁDIZ

Having repaired his battle damage and gathered reinforcements, Jervis appeared off Cádiz in early April in his new flagship, the 110-gun *Ville de Paris*. 'I thank you very much for this noble ship,' he wrote to Spencer, 'which feels like a rock after the trembling, leaky *Victory*.' At this stage, the Spanish were expected to emerge from port at any time. British intelligence had established that Mazarredo had agreed to take command again, having insisted on sweeping changes in the organization of the Royal Armada, so Jervis decided to station his fleet immediately outside the port, ready to meet the Spanish as soon as they sailed.

However, the Spanish were preoccupied with other matters. Following the fleet's ignominious arrival in Cádiz, Córdoba and his senior officers had faced a public outcry and a council of war was established to examine their conduct. At one point, it looked as if Córdoba might even be shot which horrified his former opponents, who remembered the heroic defence of the *Santissima Trinidad*. In the end, he escaped with his life but was banished from the service and from Court: as so often before, the warriors suffered for the ineptitude of their political masters.

The inshore blockading squadron off Cádiz, June 1797. This engraving, based on a drawing by Thomas Buttersworth, shows just how closely Nelson blockaded Cádiz. His flagship, HMS Theseus, *is third from the left, flying his blue admiral's flag at the mizzen.*

With the benefit of hindsight, Spanish naval historians now see the Battle of Cape St Vincent, and the demoralization that followed it, as a defining moment in the decline of the Royal Armada. In 1791, the naval registers had included 75 ships of the line; by 1802 there were only 53 of which just 29 were seaworthy.

By the middle of May, Jervis realized that the Spanish were unlikely to emerge from port unless they had a good reason. So he set about finding ways of forcing them out. First, on 19 May, he established a strict blockade. Knowing that Cádiz was the main port for most of Spain's colonial trade, and that the local economy depended on the free movement of merchant ships, he hoped that, when faced with ruination, the commercial community would bring pressure to bear on the new Spanish commander-in-chief and force him to sail. To ensure that this blockade was as effective as possible, he sent a squadron of lighter-draft battleships right into the mouth of the harbour and anchored them within sight of Cádiz town. And he gave this important and delicate command to Nelson.

This was undoubtedly one of the closest blockades of a major enemy port ever conducted by the Royal Navy. By a fortunate chance a marvellous visual record has survived in the form of a splendid series of paintings and prints by the artist

Thomas Buttersworth, who happened to be serving in the fleet at this time (see illustration on p. 95). He shows the ships so close inshore that he could well be suspected of exaggeration were his view not fully supported by the documentary evidence. On 18 April, Collingwood told his father-in-law that he was 'parading under the walls of Cádiz' and later, on 30 June, Nelson wrote to his friend the Revd Dixon Hoste 'We are looking at the ladies walking the walls and Mall of Cádiz.'

As we saw in Chapter One, Nelson had organized a similar blockade of Leghorn a year before and so he knew that he had to strike a balance between keeping a tight grip on the movement of shipping while, at the same time, doing all he could to avoid alienating the local population. He met the challenge with the same combination of firmness and friendliness which had won him respect at Leghorn. On 30 May, he sent Mazzaredo a jovial warning that the British fleet would be firing a salute on 4 June in honour of the birthday of King George III, and expressing his hope, 'that the Ladies at Cádiz may not be alarmed at the firing'. Mazzaredo replied in a similar vein, 'The Ladies of Cádiz, accustomed to the noisy sounds of salutes of the vessels of war, will sit, and will hear what Sir John Jervis means to regale them with.' But a month later, he received a much sterner note from Nelson, pointing out that some of the Spanish fishing vessels, which had hitherto been allowed to continue their work unmolested, had been 'found at such a distance from the land as plainly to evince that they have something farther in view than catching fish' and warning that if they were found outside their usual fishing ground again they would be sunk.

As at Leghorn, Nelson also managed to establish an excellent intelligence network and wrote almost daily to St Vincent with information about the Spanish fleet. For example, he allowed a 'market-boat' to sell greens to his squadron. As well as maintaining the health of his crews, this daily contact also gave him some useful information:

> the man who usually brings greens to some of the Ships here did not bring off any greens this day although particularly desired to bring plenty . . . His reason is that all the Spanish Men-of-Wars boats were on shore buying up everything; that we might think as we pleased but the Fleet was certainly coming out.

On 7 July, he was even able to tell Jervis the names of all the delegates in the latest peace talks which had started only a few weeks before in Lille. Lord Malmesbury had been sent back to reopen negotiations with an even more advantageous offer than before and, according to Nelson's informants, 'Peace is expected every day.'

We now know that the blockade was extremely effective. The number of bankruptcies in the commercial community of Cádiz increased markedly and the total loss due to capture for the period 1796–1801 has been calculated at 296 million reales – the equivalent of a whole year's exports in a normal year.

Even more significant, the British blockade led to a marked change in the make-up of the merchant fleet itself – instead of relying on the traditional, large, full-bottomed vessels, traders started to use smaller, faster ships which were more use as blockade-runners. But these economic effects took a long time to make themselves felt and so, as May dragged into June, there was still no sign of movement from the Spanish fleet .

By now, however, the British leaders had their own problems to deal with, for the first rumours of the Spithead and Nore mutinies were reaching the fleet, as ships joined from home waters. Some brought the seeds of mutiny with them but Jervis dealt with the problem with a characteristic combination of firmness and shrewd understanding that was very effective. When mutiny broke out in the *St George*, four ringleaders were tried at once and, when found guilty, were hanged the next day. This happened to be a Sunday, which brought a protest from the sabbath-observing Vice Admiral Thompson, but St Vincent was unmovable and the executions went ahead.

On the other hand, although he did not hesitate to punish severely when he thought it was deserved, Jervis did not invariably hold the seamen responsible: 'I dread not the seamen,' he wrote to Nelson on 17 June, 'it is the indiscreet, licentious conversation of the officers which produces all our ills.' So when the *Theseus* arrived in great disorder – 'an abomination' as Jervis put it to Spencer – he laid the blame for her condition squarely where it belonged and dealt with her by removing her captain and asking Miller to take command. He also asked Nelson to transfer his flag into her and, a fortnight later, a note was dropped on the *Theseus*'s quarterdeck,

> Success attend Admiral Nelson God bless Captain Miller we thank them for the officers they have placed over us. We are happy and comfortable and will shed every drop of blood in our veins to support them, and the name of the *Theseus* shall be immortalized as high as *Captain*'s.

This note was signed simply, 'Ship's company'.

The note's reference to 'the officers they have placed over us' is significant. As was customary, Nelson had taken with him a number of his young 'followers', including his two particular favourites, John Weatherhead and young William Hoste, and they had obviously been instrumental in establishing good order – helped by some old *Agamemnon*s who had also accompanied their commander. The transformation of the *Theseus* was a striking demonstration of how important it was for an eighteenth-century officer to surround himself with high-quality followers – and on the lower deck as much as in the wardroom.

By July, the continued inertia of the Spanish fleet, coupled with the need to distract the seamen from rumours of mutiny, convinced Jervis and his captains that more aggressive measures were needed, and so direct attacks on Cádiz itself were planned. As we have seen, the first, on the night of 3/4 July, was only a qualified success. The *Thunder* managed to land some shells in the town but the speed with which the Spanish flotilla reacted forced her to withdraw before she could effect any serious damage. Nelson reported to St Vincent that 'a shell fell in a Convent destroyed several priests (that no harm, they will never be missed)' and that 'plunder and robbery was going on – a glorious scene of confusion', adding, in an excited postscript, 'I open my letter to say they are all on the move.' But it was a false alarm and so, two nights later, another attempt was made.

This time, Nelson left all the arrangements to Miller and his colleague Captain Richard Bowen, one of Jervis' most favoured protégés, and they managed to get the *Thunder* into a position from which she could lob her shells into the town without being distracted by attacks from the shore. Anticipating another intervention by the Spanish gun-boats, Miller gathered the British boats together and placed them in a line between the shore and the bomb-vessel. However, the ferocity of the British counter-attack two nights before had obviously had an effect. Miller reported his opponents,

> were calling, talking to each other and making much noise, in the evident endeavour of spiriting one another up to a close decisive attack but they would come no nearer tho' they annoyed us with continual showers of shells, grape, canister and Musketry.

On returning to his ship Miller discovered that this time the *Thunder* had managed to fire forty-four shells, of which thirty-six had fallen in the town causing serious damage and loss of life.

Still there was no sign of movement from the Spanish fleet. Nelson kept probing, trying to find a weak spot. But the Spanish defence flotilla was increasing with every day that passed and when they tried another full bombardment on 10 July Miller found, 'the whole mouth of the harbour covered with launches carrying guns and other armed boats coming to assist those retiring'. Clearly, the Spanish were now so alerted to the danger, and so well prepared against it, that there was very little chance of any further attack on Cádiz having any serious effect. So, on 14 July, the inshore squadron withdrew and rejoined the main fleet. Nelson went on board the *Ville de Paris* and he and Jervis began planning their next move.

THE ORIGINS OF THE TENERIFE OPERATION

As it happened, they had a well-formed plan already to hand. In early March, while the rest of the British fleet was still refitting in the River Tagus, the newly promoted rear admiral had been sent with a small squadron to intercept the

Viceroy of Mexico, who was supposed to be approaching Cádiz from Havana with a cargo of gold reputed to be worth 6 or 7 million sterling. Like most of his contemporaries in the Royal Navy, Nelson was obsessed with the legend of rich Spanish specie ships and dreamed of a capture that would win him a fortune; but, despite a wearisome two-week patrol in the Straits, he saw no sign of this rich prize.

When he rejoined the fleet on 11 April 1797, he entertained Captain Thomas Troubridge to dinner in HMS *Captain*. Troubridge was one of his oldest friends in the Service: they had served together as midshipmen in HMS *Seahorse* in 1775 and of course they had both recently distinguished themselves at the Battle of Cape St Vincent. The rumour had reached the British fleet that the viceroy and his ships were sheltering in the Spanish Canary Islands, at the port of Santa Cruz in Tenerife, and two frigates, HMS *Terpsichore* and *Dido* had been sent to reconnoitre. Clearly, a new opportunity for action and glory was beginning to shape itself and both men wanted a share.

Following their meeting, Nelson wrote to Jervis with an outline of their joint ideas for an attack on Santa Cruz. It was a typical Nelson action-plan: full of meticulous detail demonstrating that he had done his research carefully and with a balanced analysis of the great difficulties involved and, above all, overflowing with enthusiasm for the project. In essence, what he proposed was a combined operation on very similar lines to his successful capture of Capraia the previous year: a landing by some 4,000 troops who would seize command of some heights dominating the town, while a squadron of battleships would move into a position from which they could bombard. Once these forces were in place, a demand would be sent in for the surrender of the treasure ships' cargoes. 'My plan,' he urged, 'could not fail of success, would immortalize the undertakers, ruin Spain and has every prospect of raising our Country to a higher pitch of wealth than she ever yet attained.' But just in case his admiral should suspect that the lure of Spanish gold was his main motivation, he concluded characteristically, 'But I know with you, and I can lay my hand on my heart and say the same – It is the honour and prosperity of our Country that we wish to extend.'

The letter went off to Jervis who gave it a favourable reception. But, as we have seen, the admiral had far more pressing concerns at that time, not least the need to watch the Spanish fleet in Cádiz. Moreover, the troops Nelson had mentioned were still in Porto Ferraio and so, as a first step, he was sent off to finish the evacuation of Elba. He found the convoy of troopships already on its way and escorted them safely to Gibraltar, returning to the main fleet on 24 May when he was ordered to transfer his flag to the *Theseus* and take command of the inshore squadron.

While he was away on this mission, the two scouting frigates returned. Although they had found no sign of the Viceroy of Mexico and his gold, two valuable ships had been discovered sheltering at Santa Cruz – the *San José* from

Manilla and the *Principe Fernando* from Mauritius. Under cover of darkness, the frigates sent in their boats and cut out the latter, with a cargo worth £30,000. But the *San José* still remained and she was believed to be worth ten times that sum. So the idea of a larger-scale attack remained a possibility in the minds both of Jervis and of Nelson.

By now, they knew that they would not be able to count on any help from the Army. General de Burgh had disappointed them by refusing to allow his troops to be used and a similar request to General O'Hara, Governor of Gibraltar, was also turned down. But this did not deter Nelson: on 7 June he wrote suggesting that all that was needed was an extra force of Royal Marines, 'under General Troubridge ashore, and myself afloat, I am confident of success'. Unknowing, he had taken his first step towards disaster: the attack that had originally been conceived as a large-scale combined operation, involving a significant body of trained soldiers, had now become a much smaller, and purely naval, affair.

Still Jervis continued to concentrate his attention on Cádiz and the Spanish fleet. But when, in early July, it was clear that not even Nelson's repeated bombardments were going to drive Mazarredo out of port, the Santa Cruz operation became a more attractive proposition. Not only would it result in the loss to Spain of a costly cargo, but it would also demonstrate that none of her colonies were safe from British attack: thus, Jervis hoped, increasing the growing internal opposition to the war with Britain. It was, in short, to be a classic use of seapower to bring political and economic pressure to bear on an opponent.

Intelligence from Tenerife continued to come in. Another reconnaissance, by the frigates *Lively* and *La Minerve* on 26 May, revealed that the *San José* was still anchored under the guns of Santa Cruz. The frigates succeeded in getting a close look at the chief fortifications under the pretext of delivering a letter about the exchange of prisoners and, on the night of 28/9 May, they returned under the cover of darkness and sent in a raiding party under Lieutenant Thomas Hardy to cut out a French corvette, *La Mutine* which was also sheltering there. This operation, and the previous one of April, appeared to suggest that, although Santa Cruz was strongly fortified, a well-planned full-scale attack had every chance of succeeding.

So it was that, on 14 July, Jervis recalled the inshore squadron and, following a brief discussion with Nelson, gave him orders

> for taking possession of the Town of Santa Cruz by a sudden and vigorous assault. In case of success, you are authorized to lay a heavy contribution on the inhabitants of the Town and adjacent district if they do not put you in possession of the whole cargo of *El Principe de Asturias* [sic].

He gave him a strong force: three 74-gun battleships, the *Theseus*, *Culloden* and *Zealous*, three frigates, the *Seahorse*, *Emerald* and *Terpsichore*, the cutter *Fox* and a small mortar-boat called *Terror*.

The ships were probably chosen as much for their captains as for the force they offered. For Jervis was giving Nelson the stars of his fleet: Ralph Miller, Thomas Troubridge, Sam Hood, Thomas Waller, Richard Bowen and Thomas Fremantle (whose new wife, Betsey was still with him on board the *Seahorse*). He also gave him his blessing but added a paraphrase of a famous passage from Joseph Addison's *Cato* which suggested that, even at this stage, the operation was regarded as especially difficult: 'God bless and prosper you. I am sure you will deserve success. To mortals is not given the power of commanding it.'

Don Antonio Gutiérrez,
Commandant General of
the Canary Islands.

CHAPTER EIGHT

'A sudden and vigorous assault'
The first attack

'... a series of adventures, tragic and comic, that belong to romance ...'
Captain Cuthbert Collingwood, 31 August 1797

THE SPANISH DEFENCES

Santa Cruz lies in a broad semicircular bay at the north-east tip of Tenerife. In 1797, the town was confined within a sheltered valley, with low ground immediately to its rear and rolling open ground to the south-west. To the north-east, it was protected by the sheer sides of jagged volcanic hills and could be approached only along a narrow coastal strip.

As the British frigates discovered during their reconnaissance in May, the town was strongly defended by a series of well-armed forts (see illustration on p. 104). These ran along the shore in a 6-mile line from the north-east, where a solid Martello tower, the Torre de San Andrés, stood at the foot of the mountains, to a small fort at the Barranco Hondo on the flat ground to the south-west of the town. There were sixteen individual fortifications in all, mounting a total of eighty-four guns and linked by a rough, drystone wall, running along the line of the beach. They ranged in size from the large Castillo de San Cristóbal guarding the centre of the town itself, a star-shaped sixteenth-century castle mounting ten guns, to small open-backed three- or four-gun batteries, placed at regular intervals along the beach wall.

In overall command was the Commandant General of the Canary Islands, Don Antonio Gutiérrez. A distinguished regular soldier, who had seen extensive service in earlier wars, he had been appointed to the Canaries in 1791. Although sixty-eight, he was vigorous and efficient and had done much to improve the island's defences, setting up lookout points to give early warning of attacks and reorganizing the militia.

PLAN DE LA VILLE
DE Ste. CROIX DE THÉNÉRIFE
DE SES FORTIFICATIONS

depuis la Plataforme de Passo-Alto jusqu'a
la tour ou chateau de St. Jean.
ET SA RADE
avec les principales sondes

Année 1780

Par le Chevalier Isle

EXPLICACION

1. Castillo de San Juan
2. Batería de San Francisco
3. Batería de San Telmo
4. Plataforma de la Concepción
5. Castillo de San Cristóbal
6. Batería del Rosario
7. Batería de San Pedro
8. Batería de Santa Isabel
9. Batería de San Antonio
10. Batería del Pilar
11. Espaldón de San Rafael
12. Batería de la Candelaria
13. Batería de San Miguel
14. Castillo de Paso Alto
15. Iglesia de la Concepción
16. Convento de San Francisco
17. Convento de Santo Domingo
18. Iglesia del Pilar
19. Ermita de San Telmo
20. Ermita de San Sebastián
21. Ermita de Regla
22. Hospital militar
23. Hospital de Desamparados
24. Cuartel
25. Cuerpo de guardia del muelle
26. Batería enterrada
27. Administración de Tabaco
28. Contaduría
29. Residencia del Ingeniero Jefe
30. Correo
31. Tesorería
32. Residencia del Comandante general
33. Residencia del Consul de Francia
34. Cuerpo de Guardia de Artillería
35. Antiguo hospicio de agustinos
36. Residencia del Teniente del Rey
37. Aljibe
38. Residencia del comandante de Artillería
39. Aduana
40. Cruz de mármol
41. Pila
42. Triunfo de la Candelaria
43. Cuerpo de guardia de artilleros de San Juan
44. Hornos de cal
45. Pozos
46. Aguada
47. Tejares
48. Canales

Plan of the town of Santa Cruz, 1780. The Castillo de Paso Alto, the object of Nelson's first attack on 22 July, is at the top right corner (marked 14). The second attack, on the night of 24/5 July was made in the area of the mole (see Plan IV on p. 122).

In July 1797, he had 387 gunners in the forts, only half the number required to man all his guns. In addition, he had just 400 professional soldiers, including 110 French sailors who had been stranded in Tenerife when Hardy captured *La Mutine*. In time of crisis the general could also call upon five regiments of militia, although these naturally took some time to assemble, which meant the island was very vulnerable to a sudden and determined attack. In the end, the militia call-up worked well. Over 700 men rallied to the colours and fought extremely courageously, even though most of them were armed only with sickles or sticks. Nonetheless, even at the height of the battle, Gutiérrez had only 1,669 men under his command.

THE BRITISH PREPARATIONS

Having left Jervis' fleet early on 15 June, the squadron made its way to Tenerife at a brisk pace propelled by moderate breezes from the north. This was, of course, Nelson's first major detached operation as an admiral and a distinctive feature of his style of leadership showed itself at once – full consultation with his colleagues. The captains were summoned to the *Theseus* for conferences four times: once before sailing and again on 17, 20 and 21 July and we know from Nelson's own correspondence, and from the journals of the captains themselves, that they discussed freely and openly the various options before them. In the event, the tactics they decided to employ were strikingly similar to those which had been so successful in Capraia the previous September.

First, they had to decide the exact spot where their attack was to be made. The intelligence gathered in May made it clear that the town itself was very strongly defended and so a frontal attack was not considered practical. Instead, they focused their attention on one of the outlying forts, the Castillo de Paso Alto which lay about a mile to the north-east of the town at a point where the sheer volcanic hills of Tenerife plunged precipitously into the sea. They believed that if they could gain possession of the castle, Santa Cruz's weakly defended north-eastern flank would then lie exposed and the town could be threatened with bombardment. The land forces would be supported by the battleships, which would take up a position from which they could also bombard the town. At this point, Nelson would send ashore an ultimatum demanding the surrender of the Manilla galleon and her cargo in return for sparing the inhabitants of Tenerife from 'the horrors of war'. The wording of this ultimatum was similar to the document prepared, with Sir Gilbert Elliot's assistance, for the attack on Capraia: so similar, indeed, that it seems likely that Nelson was working from a copy of the earlier document. Clearly, the experience he had gained in 1796 was being put to very good use (see note on p. 106).

Having decided on their initial objective, the actual method of capturing the castle had then to be debated. They considered two possibilities: to land further up

The Tenerife ultimatum

There is a version of the ultimatum in the British Library (BM Additional Manuscripts Nelson papers 34.906) but it is clearly a clerk's copy, since the 'signature' is in the same hand as the rest of the letter. Nicolas prints a transcription of this version (vol. II, pp. 419–20). But he also includes a facsimile of an earlier draft in Nelson's right hand and the similarities between the text of this draft and the Capraia ultimatum are very striking (see note on p. 10). It seems likely, therefore, that Nelson used the Capraia ultimatum as a model for the one he drew up at Tenerife.

Until recently, it was assumed that these were the only versions produced. However, in June 1989, a third appeared at Christie's in the 'Wolf' sale. The main text was in the same, clerkly, hand as the British Library version but with one important difference: the Wolf version had been signed by Nelson *and in his left hand* (see illustration on p. 127). Obviously then, this was the fair copy, made ready to be sent ashore at the appropriate moment and, fascinatingly, Nelson signed it *after* he had returned to the *Theseus* and after the amputation of his arm (see p. 126).

the coast to the north-east, gain possession of the heights behind the castle and then call on it to surrender; or to land on a weakly defended stretch of beach to the south-west of the castle and then turn and attack it directly. In the end, probably at the conference on 17 July, the second idea was adopted and detailed planning began.

It was decided that the frigates would go on ahead of the squadron, taking with them all the available boats and a landing force of seamen and royal marines, the latter including an extra detachment supplied by ships of the main fleet. They would then approach Tenerife under the cover of darkness and land their forces at the appointed spot at dawn. The hope was that, by this means, the castle would be surprised and captured before the Spanish had time to reinforce it.

As he and his colleagues discussed the organization of the landing, another distinctive feature of Nelson's leadership was revealed: meticulous attention to detail. Already, before leaving the fleet, he had ordered the construction of special, light scaling ladders, platforms for 18-pounder guns and a 'slay' for dragging cannon. Now, he issued a set of 'regulations' for the attack: boats were to be kept together by towing one another, thus ensuring they got on shore at the same moment; a captain was to be posted on the beach to make sure that the boats turned around quickly and made their way back to the ships to collect reinforcements and supplies; iron ramrods were to be specially made for the muskets, to replace the standard-issue wooden ones which tended to break in the heat of action and, in order further to dishearten the enemy, as many of the sailors as possible were to be dressed in spare marines' uniform coats, so as to give the impression that the landing force was made up of regular soldiers.

Most of these details were published by Nicolas in 1845 and so have featured in earlier narratives of the operation. However, Ralph Miller's recently discovered account gives some fascinating new infomation about how the landing force was actually organized:

> The whole 740 seamen were divided into three companies . . . each having a Master at Arms, or Ship's Corporal, a Boatswain's mate, and Quarter Master or Gunner's mate, an Armourer with a cold chisel, a hammer, spikes for guns, and a crow, a carpenter with a short broad axe, a heavy mall and two iron wedges, a Midshipman or mate and a Lieutenant to command it . . . These men were exercised twice a day, and tried with ball at target.

If success had depended on good planning alone, the Tenerife operation should have been a foregone conclusion.

THE FIRST LANDING: SATURDAY 22 JULY

On the morning of 21 July, the squadron lay to and, while the admiral and his captains had their last conference, the landing parties were assembled in the frigates: 200 men from the *Theseus* went in the *Seahorse*; 270 from the *Zealous* in the *Emerald* and 150 from the *Culloden* in the *Terpsichore*. Each of the frigates supplied 100 of their own men and there was also the additional marine detachment under Captain Oldfield. These brought the total to about 900 men: a formidable force indeed. The complicated transfer took most of the day but eventually, at about 1600, the heavily laden frigates parted company towing all the extra boats behind them.

Left behind in his denuded flagship – as well as the 200 seamen and marines, Miller and four of his six lieutenants were with the landing party – Nelson now had to endure the strain of waiting while others carried out his plans. Giving the frigates about three hours start, he then made his own way to Tenerife with the battleships, arriving in sight of the town at about 0430 on 22 July.

There, instead of a landing in full progress, he found the boats still more than a mile from their objective. Despite all their careful planning, Nelson and his colleagues had been thwarted at the first throw by one element for which they could not plan: the weather. Between May and September, the trade winds, known as the *alisios*, blow in Tenerife. To the north of Santa Cruz – exactly where the British landing was supposed to take place – these winds blow with considerable

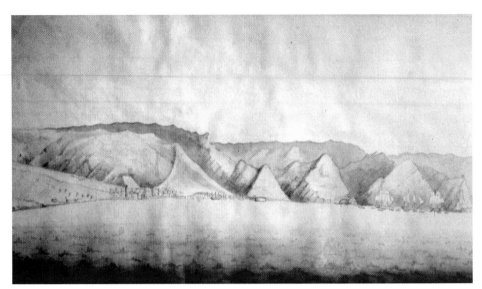

The first British attack, 22 July 1797. This watercolour, painted on the spot by Lieutenant William Webly of HMS Zealous, *shows the British squadron on the right, surrounded by boats. In the centre, is the distinctive conical shape of La Altura, with the Castillo de Paso Alto at its foot.*

force down gullies in the volcanic ranges, creating gusts and swirls and whipping up the sea into what the Tenerife fishermen call 'the white sheet'. The boats' progress had been slowed to such an extent that the element of surprise had been lost and, even as Nelson watched, three shots were fired in the town, showing that his force had been spotted. Within moments, Gutiérrez had been alerted to the danger and had begun to make his countermeasures. An aide was sent off to Laguna, 5 miles inland, to call up the militia and, in the meantime, the general sent all his available forces – including the French sailors – to occupy the heights of La Altura, above the Castillo de Paso Alto.

Briefly, the attack hung in the balance. The Spanish reinforcements would take time to reach their positions and so there was still a chance that the British could establish a foothold if they pushed on quickly. Instead, at the first signs of Spanish activity, Troubridge ordered his boats to return to the shelter of the frigates while, with Bowen and Oldfield, he rowed out to the *Theseus* to consult with Nelson. The whole momentum of the British attack was lost.

All authorities have agreed it is extraordinary that Troubridge, the man who had led the British fleet so steadfastly into action at Cape St Vincent, should have faltered at this critical moment. Naturally, he could not have known that the forces opposing him were so weak but, even so, he should have realized that a bold drive ahead offered his only hope of success. However, we now know that Troubridge was far from well – according to Miller he had 'lately been very ill' – and so it is possible that he was simply below par. Whatever the reason, by hesitating when he did, he threw away the one real chance of a British victory.

Arriving on board the *Theseus* at about 0600 Troubridge and his colleagues conferred with Nelson. They now revived the other option they had considered earlier: to occupy the heights above the fort and then storm it from the rear. A convenient landing beach was available close to the frigates, at the mouth of the Barranco del Bufadero, and from there it appeared a relatively easy climb to the ridge above the fort. Nelson gave his assent to the plan and between about 1000 and 1030, the boats left the frigates for a second time. In the meantime, the battleships tried to create a diversion by attacking the fort but were unable to get within range because of light winds and contrary currents. The mortar-boat *Terror* was sent in to try lobbing her shells but she was unable to get close enough to be accurate.

So, the sailors began toiling at their oars once again and this time the landing party got ashore. Slowly, they laboured up the slope of the Jurada heights, which Miller later described as, 'a tremendous hill without a path and full of rocks and loose stones'. As the day progressed, the sun grew ever hotter and they had very little food and water with them, since an attack of this duration had not been envisaged. But eventually, 'excessively fatigued', they reached the top of the slope – only to find another setback awaiting them.

The battle site today, showing the difficult terrain which Troubridge encountered. From left to right are: the dark, triangular shape of La Altura on which the Spanish defenders were entrenched; the deep gully of the Valleseco; and the Jurada heights, up which the British attackers toiled.

Seen from the ships, the Jurada appeared a continuous part of the heights overlooking the castle. But now, as they stood on the ridge, the British saw that there was in fact a deep valley – the Valleseco – between them and their objective. And there, firmly entrenched behind a rough wall on the opposite ridge, were the Spanish defenders, the Regiment of the Militia of La Laguna, who had even managed to carry four field pieces on their shoulders up the steep hillside. General Gutiérrez's hastily assembled forces had reached their posts in time.

It must have been an appalling moment for the unfortunate Troubridge. Just when success seemed within his grasp, it was snatched away again. To attack the Spaniards, his men would first have to descend into the deep valley and then fight their way up the bare rocky slope on the other side in the face of plunging fire from the well-entrenched defenders. And by now his men were 'much fatigued and in want of refreshment', as his own log put it. Worst of all was the heat. The islanders were used to the climate and, in any case, behind their lines women and children were carrying food and water up to their menfolk; but the British had very little water. One of the defenders, Bernardo Cólogan, a Spanish officer of Irish descent, later recorded sympathetically, 'they were dying of thirst . . . in those mountains there were no areas where they could take shelter from the blazing sun and there was not a breath of wind to bring some relief'. Some of the sailors tried to get down into the Valleseco, where there was a little brackish water, but two were shot, one died of exhaustion as he tried to struggle back up the hill to join his comrades and some of the others who had actually drunk the water fell down senseless. A few ripe grapes were found which gave some relief, but they were not enough to refresh the whole party.

Eventually, Troubridge accepted defeat and ordered a retreat, which was carried out in reasonable order. First went the sick and those suffering from heat exhaustion; then the main force beat to arms, to give the Spanish the impression they were about to attack, and began to move off in companies, with the marines bringing up the rear in case of a counter-attack. By 2200, the whole force had been re-embarked in the frigates, worn out and in an extremely bad temper: 'The *Theseus*'s men the most tiresome, noisy, mutinous people in the world', Betsey Fremantle noted when they returned to the *Seahorse*. Their anger was understandable: the British attack had ended in ignominious – indeed, almost comic – failure.

THE COUNCIL OF WAR

On Sunday 23 July, the wind freshened to a gale from the north-east and for the next twenty-four hours no further operations were possible as the ships were forced to keep tacking to and fro to avoid being driven ashore. Nelson was extremely frustrated. His natural instinct was to lead from the front and now he had been forced to witness from a distance the failure of two assaults under his

The first British attack: the Spanish view. As General Gutiérrez and his staff watch from the walls of the Castillo de San Cristóbal (right), the British squadron anchors to the north-east of the town. In the foreground, members of the militia are given their orders, while some of the general's regulars reinforce the defences of the mole with field guns.

overall direction. Doubts began to set in: as he wrote later to his friend Sir Andrew Snape Hammond, 'Had I been with the first party, I have reason to believe complete success would have crowned our endeavours.' Nonetheless, by any reasonable standard, he had done all he could to carry out his orders: winds, and other natural obstacles beyond his control were mainly responsible for his failure and he would therefore have been perfectly justified in sailing away without making any further attempt. Instead, within twenty-four hours he was not only leading a second attack in person but was also making it in the most hazardous manner possible – a direct, frontal assault on the centre of the town itself.

Various attempts have been made to explain this decision. Nelson himself said in his letter to Hammond, '. . . My pride suffered . . .' and so it has been suggested that he was acting more out of a sense of wounded personal honour than of cool evaluation. There is also an idea that he was simply overconfident – believing after his remarkable exploits at Cape St Vincent, and outside Cádiz that he was a match for any Spaniard. However, Miller's newly discovered account presents a rather different picture.

During the retreat in the evening of 22 July, a deserter from Santa Cruz was brought aboard the *Seahorse* by Captain Oldfield and the following morning he was interrogated by Miller and Fremantle. He was a Prussian and, according to Miller, Betsey Fremantle (like all her sisters, a good linguist) acted as interpreter for them. Although Betsey herself does not mention this fact in her own journal, she left a very vivid record of the deserter's words, which suggests that she knew exactly what was said:

> A German that was brought off yesterday says the Spaniards have no force, are in the greatest alarm, all crying and trembling, and that nothing could be easier than to take the place, only 300 men of regular troops, the rest are peasants who are frightened to death.

Miller echoes Betsey's words, 'He assured us we might easily take it' and then goes on to give a fascinating insight into how the decision to renew the attack was reached:

> . . . we agreed that Fremantle should carry the information and talk to the Admiral on it (as nobody generally has less influence with an Admiral than his Captain) and endeavour to bring him on board the *Seahorse* as there was no person in the squadron could interpret half so well as Mrs Fremantle. He accordingly went on board the *Theseus* and soon after the signal was made 'for All Captains' and a council of war was held. The result of which was to storm the Town.

So we now know that the decision to make the second attack was not arrived at by Nelson in isolation, but was in fact urged on him by his captains at a full council of war and based on apparently good intelligence. We also know that, shortly after the council had decided to attempt another attack, Nelson received additional intelligence which increased his confidence still further. On the morning of 24 July, Captain Thomas Thompson arrived in HMS *Leander*. He knew Tenerife well from previous visits and his local knowledge of the actual layout of the town of Santa Cruz meant that Nelson could make his detailed plans for the attack with some precision.

These new insights into the way the second attack at Tenerife was decided upon give us a fascinating glimpse of Nelson learning to be an admiral. We can now see that past suggestions that his decisions were based on overconfidence and personal

Nelson in 1797. This watercolour, painted by one of Nelson's officers, possibly during the blockade of Cádiz, shows him before his dangerous wound prematurely aged him – still plump-cheeked and youthful: even with a trace of a double-chin! The pen, and the drawing in front of him, are later additions.

pride are unfair. If there is a criticism that can be levelled at him it is, perhaps, a more subtle one: that he was not detached enough; too eager, like his captains, to find a reason for renewing the attack. He was, of course, the same age as them, which must have made detachment particularly difficult. This is vividly shown in a revealing image of him, dating from about this time – a watercolour drawing, possibly painted by one of his officers in the *Theseus*, and now preserved in the Nelson Museum at Monmouth (see p. 113). It depicts a very youthful man: the face still plump and boyish; the eyes staring straight ahead intently; the body tensed like a well-trained setter. He looks more like a keen young lieutenant than an experienced flag-officer.

Nelson did not mention the crucial council of war in his official dispatch – which is why the older accounts have tended to place the blame entirely on him. Miller's account enables us to redress the balance and, as a result, Nelson emerges from the Tenerife operation with honour. Having taken the decision to attack, he accepted full responsibility for the ensuing failure and, even in the depths of his depression following his disabling wound, made no attempt to shift the blame.

PLANNING THE SECOND ATTACK

The shoreline of Santa Cruz was mainly rocky and inhospitable and there was no natural harbour or anchorage. To counter this, the Spanish had constructed a short mole, founded on a tongue of larva that stretched out into the sea, directly opposite the main square of the town (see Plan IV on p. 122). To the south and west, the rocky shore made landings impossible; but on the north side of the mole was a small sheltered beach. Two sets of steps gave access to a wide platform on the top of the mole, from which a gate in the shore wall led to the main square. At the mole's seaward end was a small semicircular battery, mounting seven guns; at its landward end, it was defended by the citadel, the Castillo de San Cristóbal, whose outer walls were actually bedded into the mole itself. Most of the castle's ten guns had arcs of fire that could sweep the mole from end to end (see illustration on p. 120).

It was a formidable position; and yet it was precisely there that Nelson now proposed to aim his attack, relying on being able to land sufficient men to overwhelm the defences. He did plan one feint. In an attempt to deceive Gutiérrez about his true intentions, he proposed to anchor the squadron off the Barranco del Bufadero, scene of the abortive landing on 22 July, and hoist out the boats again, as if another attack on the Castillo de Paso Alto was contemplated. Miller ordered his carpenter, sail maker and cooper to make a dummy 18-pounder gun, out of barrel hoops and black-painted canvas, which was then to be laboriously lowered into a boat to lend colour to the impression that a full-scale assault on the castle was intended. But the weather continued so squally that the diversion could not take place and, although the general did send some troops to reinforce the outlying castle, he kept most of his forces along the main defensive line, while he remained in his main headquarters at the citadel. Far from being 'all crying and trembling', the garrison of Santa Cruz was now thoroughly on the alert and every available man was at his post. The chances of achieving any kind of surprise were minimal.

The practical details of Nelson's plan were simple. Once again, his seamen and marines, reinforced by a detachment from the *Leander*, were to land from the squadron's boats, with a reserve of some 200 men carried in the *Fox* cutter. The men were divided into six divisions: five under Captains Troubridge, Miller, Waller, Hood and the newly arrived Thompson respectively and the sixth under Nelson's personal command with Captains Fremantle and Bowen 'to regulate the attack'. All were to land on the mole and rendezvous in the square behind the citadel, which was then to be stormed. In other words, Nelson was concentrating all his available forces for a knockout blow on Gutiérrez's headquarters, in the hope of paralysing the Spanish defences by eliminating their command centre.

Certainly, it was a high-risk plan and, far from being overconfident, it is clear that everyone in the British squadron was well aware of the odds against them. Nelson later told Hammond, 'I felt the second attack a forlorn hope' and all the evidence is that his comrades felt the same way. Miller spent the waiting time inspecting his men, 'saw that all were perfectly sober and said a few words of encouragement to them, and caution against straggling, plundering or injuring any person not found in arms'. Elsewhere, wills were made, last letters were written. In the flagship young Lieutenant Josiah Nisbet was summoned to the admiral's cabin to help his stepfather to sort and burn Lady Nelson's letters. Josiah's warlike appearance indicated that he was preparing to join the landing party and Nelson tried to dissuade him, 'Should we both fall Josiah, what would become of your poor mother?' Josiah staunchly resisted and within a few hours he was to save Nelson's life.

Amidst all these grim preparations there was one lighter interlude in HMS *Seahorse*, when Betsey Fremantle gave a supper party for the admiral and some of his captains. Whatever their personal fears may have been, the men obviously took pains to keep them from Betsey, for she went to bed convinced that 'the taking of the place seemed an easy and almost a sure thing'.

Nelson wounded at Tenerife. William Bromley based his version of the event on earlier, inaccurate accounts which said that Nelson had actually landed on the mole when he was wounded. It later emerged that he never left the boat. Nonetheless, like all Bromley's illustrations, this is a vivid and realistic impression of the scene.

CHAPTER NINE

'A forlorn hope'
The night attack

'I believe more daring intrepidity was never shown.'
Nelson's official letter to Lord St Vincent, 27 July 1797

THE ATTACK ON THE MOLE

At dusk, the mortar-boat *Terror* approached the Castillo de Paso Alto and began a bombardment, in order to reinforce the idea that the next attack would be made there. In the meantime, the British sailors and marines began embarking in their boats once again. They had been ordered to rendezvous around HMS *Zealous* at 2230, where they were formed into their six divisions and roped together. Then, with their oars muffled, they began the 2-mile row to the mole, accompanied by the cutter *Fox*, with the reserves on board.

The *Seahorse*'s barge led the way, with Nelson and Fremantle in the sternsheets. With them was the Prussian deserter, who was being taken along 'as a guide', according to William McPherson, gunner's mate of the *Seahorse*, who added that the assault on the mole was 'conterary to the advise of the guide or pilot'. So it would seem that, now he was actually taking part, the unfortunate man was beginning to regret his earlier enthusiasm for another attack. Apparently, he did not survive.

'It was a star light, yet not a clear night,' says Miller, 'with little wind and a swell that became considerable as we approached the shore.' As a result the flotilla managed to get closer to their objective without being discovered than they had dared hope. But eventually they were spotted by a lookout in the battery on the molehead and others in the vessels lying nearby. The alarm bell rang and the whole of the Santa Cruz front burst into flame as the guns roared out. Immediately, with a concerted cheer, the boats cast off their connecting ropes and each made their own way to the mole. But in the darkness and confusion, only five – mostly those of Nelson's division – found it.

First ashore was Bowen, with a party of about fifty men. Landing on the beach just to the north of the mole, they managed to establish a foothold on the molehead itself, capturing the battery and spiking its seven guns. They then regrouped, ready to storm and capture the landward defences of the mole – but, by now, the strength of those defences was becoming all too apparent. The whole length of the mole was being swept by gunfire from the citadel, supported by musketry from nearby houses; while, to the east the Rosario and San Pedro batteries were keeping up a flanking fire. And, to reinforce this concentrated firepower, the Spanish had brought up a battery of field guns which they placed close to the gateway leading to the square, with their barrels pointing straight down the mole.

Now a second and larger British wave, including Fremantle's barge, arrived on the beach. Fremantle leapt out and began running to the mole, his men close behind him. The barge was a large boat, so it took some time to empty. Nelson had reached the middle and was in the act of drawing his sword, prior to leaping down on to the beach, when he suddenly felt a sharp blow to his elbow and his whole arm went limp. A musket ball had entered just above the joint, shattering the bone and severing a major artery. It was a very dangerous and potentially mortal wound.

Luckily for Nelson, Josiah Nisbet was still at his side. In the light of the nearby gun flashes, he saw his stepfather stagger and heard the words, 'I am shot through the elbow' as the admiral collapsed into the bottom of the boat. As he fell, Nelson still had the presence of mind to switch his sword to his left hand: it was a family heirloom passed to him by his uncle and patron, Captain Maurice Suckling. The blood was pumping fast from the wound and so Nisbet found the place where it was broken and

'Sir Horatio Nelson when wounded at Tenerife' by Richard Westall. Although Westall was able to base this illustration for Clarke and M'Arthur's biography on precise information supplied by Fanny Nelson, he nonetheless could not resist creating yet another sanitized, 'heroic' image. For a more accurate impression of the confusion and desperation of the moment, see the painting by William Bromley on p. 116.

Where was Nelson wounded?

There are two traditions about the exact location of Nelson's wounding. In the biographical essay in volume III of the *Naval Chronicle*, published just three years after the event, it was stated that he had actually left the boat and was advancing along the mole when he was struck. This version found its way into the biography by T.O. Churchill (1808) and was illustrated by William Bromley, who produced a very realistic image, now in the Royal Naval Museum, of the wounded admiral, his arm roughly bandaged, being lifted back into the boat by Josiah and a sailor (see illustration on p. 116).

However, this version of the event was contradicted first by Emma Hamilton and then by Fanny Nelson, both of whom were convinced that Nelson was still in the boat, and in the act of stepping out of it, when he was hit. In his 1806 biography, Harrison claims that his account, 'most assuredly proceeded from the ever to be revered hero's own faithful lips' (vol. I, p. 218) – which probably means that he heard it from Emma. Fanny's own memorandum on the incident, written in about 1806 for Clarke and M'Arthur, has survived and she says quite specifically, 'In the act of Sir H. putting his foot over the boat, he was shot thro' the elbow.' (Naish, pp. 374–5.) Clarke and M'Arthur faithfully reported this version in their biography and it was illustrated, albeit in a rather improbably heroic style, by Richard Westall (see illustration opposite).

These authoritative statements are supported by other primary evidence. For example, Betsey Fremantle's diary entry reads, 'The Admiral was wounded as he was getting out of the boat.' (Fremantle, vol. II, p. 185) and Miller, in his newly discovered account says, 'the Admiral had reached the middle of the boat, and was drawing his sword to jump on shore when a musket ball shattered the bone of his right arm'.

Miller's reference to 'the middle of the boat' has the ring of eyewitness authenticity about it and so it has been incorporated into the narrative.

grasped hard with one hand to stop the flow. Then using a couple of neckerchiefs, he tied up the wound. Nelson always acknowledged that Nisbet's prompt action saved his life; in her notes about the incident, written in 1806 for Clarke and M'Arthur, Lady Nelson recalled, 'Lord Nelson said in ten minutes he was no more.'

Meanwhile, the rest of the force that had reached the beach by the mole was pinned down by the Spanish fire. Fremantle and his men tried to join up with Bowen on the mole but, before they could do so, Fremantle was also hit in the arm. Thompson landed just at that moment and told his own boat to take his wounded colleague back to the *Seahorse*, while he tried to force his way forward. Then he too was hit. Meanwhile, Bowen, having rallied his men at the molehead and ordered them to reload, had just begun a charge down the mole towards the citadel when the Spanish field pieces opened fire with a murderous blast of cannister shot, cutting a swathe through his small force. Bowen and his first lieutenant, George Thorpe, were killed outright, together with six of their men and a number of the rest were wounded.

Thus, in the space of about ten minutes, the Spanish had succeeded in knocking out all the British leaders on the mole. So furious and effective was this sudden hail of fire, that Nelson later calculated that his landing force had been opposed to '30 or 40 pieces of cannon', with '4 or 500 men' manning them. But the Spanish sources show that there were fewer than twenty guns in this area and less than a hundred men. As Agustín Guimerá has pointed out in his definitive account of the battle from the Spanish point of view, 'the ravages caused by the guns were not due to their number as Nelson claims but to the careful positioning'. The mole and the adjoining beach were so narrow that a few well-aimed guns, loaded with cannister, could easily pin down the small force that had actually managed to land.

The mole at Santa Cruz, showing the strength of the position Nelson was attacking. On the right is the main citadel, the Castillo de San Cristóbal, while flanking fire came from two batteries just out of the picture on the left. The beach on which Nelson's force landed is in the left foreground.

The only way in which the British could have carried such a strong position would have been by a concentrated landing of a much larger party. Such indeed had been Nelson's intention: but his desperate attempt had been frustrated by the heavy swell and darkness. Miller says that 'it was so dark near the shore that without going close to them you could not discern objects with any precision' and, as a result, most of the landing force was swept past the mole towards the southern part of the town. According to Miller, some of the boats gave up the attempt altogether, daunted by the fierceness of the fire and the heavy swell which was pounding the rocks. But some actually managed to get ashore.

THE LANDINGS IN THE TOWN

First ashore was Troubridge's division, which fetched up on the Aduana beach, just a few yards south of the citadel, together with some of the *Emerald*'s division under Waller (see Plan IV on p. 122). Their boats were either swamped by the breakers, or stove in on the rocks and all their powder was soaked; but they nonetheless charged with bayonets and pikes and drove away the defenders, who were all inexperienced militiamen. They then ran for cover into the nearest street, the Calle de la Caleta, and eventually, probably guided by the firing from the mole, emerged into the main square at its upper end.

Their next action should have been to attack the citadel from its landward side, thus supporting the attack on the mole. But their ammunition was wet and they had lost their scaling ladders when their boats were wrecked on the rocks. All they could do therefore was wait, in the hope that Nelson and his division would gain control of the mole and then come and join them. The long moments went by and then, suddenly, they were spotted from the citadel and fired upon. So they took shelter in a convenient warehouse.

This was a worrying moment for Gutiérrez. Until then, his attention had been wholly taken up with the battle below him on the mole; but now he learned that a British detachment had been spotted in his rear, at the upper end of the square, and that his communications with his right flank to the south had been cut. He probably began to suspect that the attack on the mole was simply a feint, intended to occupy him, while the main British force landed in the town itself and then marched to take him in the rear. Certainly, he at once sent out orders to his outlying forces, ordering them to concentrate on the citadel; which suggests that he feared a major assault on his command position.

Slowly, the minutes ticked by and the tension mounted. Then, quite unexpectedly, a flag of truce arrived at the castle gates, accompanied by two Spanish gentlemen and a sergeant of marines who brought with them a demand from Troubridge for the surrender of the citadel. Unable to take any direct offensive action, he had decided to try a bluff. But he was up against an experienced professional, who was not easily cowed. Gutiérrez disdained even to reply to the summons and gave orders for the envoys to be detained.

PLAN IV

SANTA CRUZ DE TENERIFE
The British landings
25 July 1797

KEY

1. The Mole
2. Mole Battery
3. Castillo de San Cristóbal
4. Rosario Battery
5. The Mole Beach
6. Main town square
7. Aduana Beach
8. Warehouse in which Troubridge's force took shelter
9. Concepción battery
10. Aciete gully
11. Carnicería beach
12. Barranco de Santos
13. Igelsia de la Concepción
14. Convento de Santo Domingo

A. Landing place of the main force: Nelson, Bowen, Fremantle, Thompson

B. Landing place of Troubridge's force

C. Landing place of Miller and Hood's force

D. Place where remainder of landing force was repulsed

Still the British were coming ashore in small, disorganized groups (see Plan IV opposite). According to the Spanish accounts, a group of boats drifted right to the south of the town, where the Barranco de Santos offered a convenient landing place. But Gutiérrez had foreseen that this might be chosen as the point of attack and so he had posted his most experienced troops there, the Infantry Batallion of the Canaries, made up of 227 men and supported by 120 militiamen. As the boats approached, these soldiers opened up a well-organized fire on them and succeeded in driving them away. Until now, it has been assumed that these boats were Miller's and Hood's; but Miller's newly discovered account, which is very detailed and honest, makes no mention of this repulse and so it is likely that this was another and quite separate British contingent. We know that at least 200 men from the landing party did not get ashore at all; so it seems reasonable to assume that it was this group that was repulsed at the Barranco de Santos.

Miller, in the *Theseus*'s pinnace, supported by Captain Oldfield in her launch, did succeed in landing, in a small gully known as Barranquillo del Aciete, close to the Concepción battery. Their boats grounded in the heavy surf about 30 yards from the shore and began to fill with water so they were forced to wade to the beach, with the water chest-high. Although under fire from more of Gutiérrez's professionals, about sixty men of the Banderas de La Habana y Cuba, they managed to drive their opponents out of the battery with a pike charge. At this point they were joined by Captain Sam Hood with another group, making a total force of about forty or fifty men. Having gained this foothold, Miller and Hood tried to rally their men for an attack on the citadel but they found that, by now, morale was very low. Most of their powder was wet and some of them had actually lost their arms in the struggle to get ashore; moreover they had already suffered heavy casualties and so, says Miller frankly, 'as a body [they] behaved indifferently through the night'. The few marines present seemed prepared to advance but, despite all Miller's efforts and those of his officers, the sailors could not be persuaded to make what was obviously a desperate attack.

Given the situation in which they found themselves, such hesitation is wholly understandable – and indeed Miller himself admitted later that he was not surprised. For the British were now in a serious predicament. Their planned concerted attack on a single point had disintegrated into a series of uncoordinated landings and there were now three separate British groups ashore, none of which was in touch with the others. It was still pitch dark and they were now confronted with a confusing maze of narrow, winding streets filled with the dark forms of Spanish defenders moving towards the main square, in response to Gutiérrez's earlier order to concentrate on the citadel. A series of scrappy, bewildering skirmishes broke out in which the defenders – with their local knowledge and plentiful supplies of ammunition – had a considerable advantage.

Abandoning their idea of attacking the citadel, Hood and Miller now tried to reach the agreed rendezvous in the main square. They blundered about in the dark, meeting first some more British who had just landed and then another party of Spaniards who melted away into the nearby dark alleyways. Finally, they found themselves in the square in front of the Church of the Concepción, where they regrouped their disorganized force, 'and the strictest caution was given to officers and men against straggling, entering the houses, pillaging or hurting any they met without arms'. Then they plunged once again into the narrow winding streets, trying to link up with their comrades; but they missed the way to the main square and ended up, instead, outside the Convento de Santo Domingo with the Spanish closing in behind them. By now they were taking casualties from 'the inhabitants firing at us from holes and corners'. One of these was Bernardo Cólogan who later wrote,

> Our people threw themselves into all the alley-mouths leading to these streets, in bands of from forty to sixty soldiers, some of them having a field gun discharging grape. As soon as the enemy showed his face, these were fired and felled a number of them.

Somehow, a message had got through to Troubridge that the other party had landed and so, realizing his position in the square was hopeless, he retreated towards his colleagues and finally succeeded in joining up with them outside the convent. This was an excellent defensive position: a large, square two-storied building with no ground-floor windows and a bell-tower with a convenient balcony, from which they could look out over the roofs of the neighbouring buildings. They seized it and, using ammunition they had captured from the various Spanish detachments overwhelmed earlier, kept the encircling forces at bay.

Troubridge and his fellow captains now realized that their position was very serious. Although by concentrating their forces, they had managed to gather together some 340 men, they did not have enough ammunition to fight a serious action with the ever-increasing forces that were now surrounding them. So, instead, they tried another bluff. Captain Oldfield was sent with a flag of truce with a threat to burn the town, unless the Manilla galleon was surrendered. He was admitted with due ceremony to the citadel but Gutiérrez had now begun to realize that he had the upper hand; he refused to negotiate and Oldfield returned to the convent. Next, two friars were sent and the British made sure that, before they left the convent, they got a good view of the preparations that were under way for firing the town. As Collingwood later told the story, 'In the presence of the priests they were employed in preparing torches, fire-balls, and all the necessary apparatus for conflagration; and they in terror fled to the Governor to entreat him to grant those mad Englishmen any terms by which they might get rid of them.' Still Gutiérrez remained unmoved.

At last, having tried every trick they could think of, the British accepted defeat. In his official report to Nelson, Troubridge claimed that he marched again on the citadel and only negotiated when he realized how many troops had been concentrated against him. But none of the Spanish sources mention this sortie and it would seem that he was exaggerating a little. What is certain is that Hood now made his way to the citadel and, for the first time, offered to discuss a British capitulation, although he still continued to threaten to burn the town if honourable terms were not offered. Given that he had the upper hand, Gutiérrez could afford to be generous and he agreed to allow his opponents to leave with full military honours, even keeping their arms. In return, Hood promised that his forces and the ships of the squadron 'shall not molest the Town in any manner . . . or any of the Islands of the Canaries'. Troubridge ratified these terms and, by 0700 on 25 July, the hostilities were finally over.

NELSON'S ARM IS AMPUTATED

What, meanwhile, of Nelson? Having staunched the flow of blood from his stepfather's shattered elbow, Nisbet gathered a scratch crew together and refloated the heavy barge, which was firmly aground on the beach. They began the long journey back to the ships, running close inshore so as to keep under the trajectory of the guns in the various batteries, which were still blazing away. As his initial shock began to ebb, Nelson asked to be lifted up so that he could look around him. In the middle of this hazardous voyage – Lady Nelson later remembered her son speaking of 'heavy fire and tempestuous sea the spray from the shot coming [into the boat]' – there came a sudden loud cry. The cutter *Fox*, still being towed slowly towards the mole ready to land her reinforcements, had been hit by a 24-pounder shot, which went right through her at the waterline. At once, she filled and began to sink like a stone, tipping her packed occupants into the water and, despite his stepson's protests, Nelson insisted on stopping to rescue some of the drowning men.

The first ship they reached was the *Seahorse*; but Nelson refused to go on board, for fear of alarming Betsey Fremantle. When they arrived at the *Theseus*, willing hands tried to help him on board. 'Let me alone,' came the reply, 'I have yet my legs left and one arm' and so, as young William Hoste who had been left on board later wrote to his father,

> I beheld him, who I may say has been a second father to me, his right arm dangling by his side while with the other he helped himself jump up the ship's side, and with great spirit which astonished every one, told the surgeon to get his instruments ready for he knew he must lose his arm and that the sooner it was off the better. He underwent the operation with the same firmness and courage that have always marked his character.

Who cut off Nelson's arm?

In all the confusion of this most confused event even the identity of the surgeon who amputated Nelson's arm has been the subject of some debate. For many years, an 'operating saw' was displayed in the old Royal United Services Institute Museum, purporting to be the 'Saw with which Dr Auchmuty amputated Lord Nelson's arm in 1797.' But in fact the surgeon of the *Theseus* was Thomas Eshelby and he had two surgeon's mates to help him: Louis Remonier, a French royalist refugee from the hospital at Toulon, who had been allowed to join the Royal Navy and nineteen-year-old George Henderson, who went with the landing parties and was drowned during the abortive attack on the mole.

Some of Nelson's biographers suggest that it was Remonier who actually performed the amputation. However, an 'Account of Admiral Nelson's expenses attending the cure of his wound' has survived and is published in Naish (p. 378). Here, Remonier's fee (£25 4s 0d) is stated as being for 'assisting in amputating my arm and attendance from 25th July 1797 to the 17th August following during which he sat up 14 nights', while Eshelby's (£36 0s 0d) is for 'amputating my arm and attending me to England in the *Seahorse* frigate'. So, it was definitely Eshelby who performed the actual operation.

In passing, it is interesting to note that this expenses sheet shows that eighteenth-century naval surgeons were allowed to supplement their income with special charges.

Despite this stoical outward front, Nelson always retained an unpleasant memory of the first shock of the cold knife cutting into his flesh. Some years later, he instructed George Magrath, the surgeon of the *Victory*, to make sure that warm water was always available in the cockpit to warm the instruments before use.

Nelson now showed the remarkable powers of recovery which he was to demonstrate again at the Nile. According to Collingwood, 'in half an hour after [his arm] was off he gave all orders necessary for carrying on their operations as if nothing had happened to him'. He even made his first very shaky attempt at writing his name left-handed, signing a copy of the ultimatum he had intended to send ashore demanding the surrender of the Manilla galleon's cargo in return for sparing the town (see illustration opposite). Quite why he did so at this stage is not clear: perhaps he had received news that Troubridge and his colleagues had managed to get ashore and wanted to have the ultimatum ready to send to Gutiérrez, should they prove successful.

> I Allow half of One Hour
> for Acceptance or Rejection –
>
> To,   Horatio Nelson
> The Governor or Command.
> Officer at Santa Cruz

> God Bless You & Fremantle
>
> Horatio Nelson

> y will be able to give me a frigate to convey the
> remains of my carcase to England, God Bless
> You my Dear Sir & Believe me your
> most Obliged & faithful
>
> Horatio Nelson
>
> You will excuse my scrawl
> considering it is my first Attempt

Nelson's first left-handed writing. From top to bottom:
a) His first signature (on a copy of the British ultimatum) written very shortly
after the amputation in the early hours of 25 July – note how it has taken him two
attempts to get used to writing with his left hand.
b) His first note, written to Betsey Fremantle sometime on 26 July.
c) His first full letter, written to Sir John Jervis on 27 July.

In fact, of course, the ultimatum was never sent; for as first light dawned, the extent of the disaster could be seen and the bad news began to arrive from the shore. At the same time, the Castillo de Paso Alto began firing on the ships, so they had to get under way quickly, despite being very short-handed; the *Theseus*, with her captain still on shore and her admiral incapacitated, was forced to cut her cable. Slowly, they worked their way to the north-east, only to find themselves coming within range of the Torre de San Andrés whose guns now came into action for the first time, firing the last shots of the battle. Even as they did so, a messenger came galloping along the coast road to tell the Spanish gunners that a truce had been declared.

THE BRITISH SURRENDER

Back in the town, the formal surrender procedures were already under way. With colours flying, the British marched down from the convent to the main square, where all the available Spanish troops had been drawn up in orderly lines. Gutiérrez had decided to make an impressive show of strength in the hope of deterring the British from making any further attacks. His men were also busily spreading the rumour that there were 8,000 troops on the island – a figure not unnaturally seized on first by Troubridge, and then by Nelson, as an explanation for their humiliating defeat. Both quoted this figure in their reports and, as a result, it has featured in most British accounts of the battle since. But the Spanish sources are quite clear on this point: Gutiérrez had at his disposal only the 1,669 men mentioned earlier. The figure of 8,000 was the parting propaganda shot of a wily opponent.

As the British came into the square, they spotted that the French sailors had also been drawn up to watch them pass and Troubridge protested angrily until he was assured by the Spanish that there was 'no thought of an Insult'. Indeed, Gutiérrez continued to be generous in victory. When the British found that they could not re-embark easily because most of their boats had been destroyed, he supplied two local barquentines to assist with the ferrying. The wounded were taken to a Spanish hospital; the weary attackers were given bread and wine and Troubridge, Hood and Miller, having turned down a courteous invitation to breakfast, were offered lemonade and cake. The refreshments were very welcome, for by then the three captains 'were parched with heat and thirst and the dirt on our wet cloaths had form'd a perfect crust'.

These courtesies were reported to Nelson and, quick to recognize a kindred spirit, he sent Gutiérrez a present of some English beer and a cheese on 26 July. With them, went an appreciative letter offering 'my sincerest thanks for your attention to Myself and your humanity to those of our wounded who were in your possession or under your care as well as your generosity to all that were landed'. (See Appendix 2 on p. 160 for full text of the letter.) At the bottom, was another of Nelson's new left-handed signatures and, at some time during that day, he also made his first wavering attempt at putting together a sequence of words. Characteristically, it was a note of encouragement to Betsey Fremantle, reading simply, 'God Bless You and Fremantle Horatio Nelson' (see illustration on p. 127). According to Surgeon Eshelby's notes, his patient was by now 'quite easy' and was on a regimen of fluids: 'Tea, Soup, and Sago. Lemonade and Tamarind Drink.'

Gutiérrez replied to Nelson's letter with one equally appreciative, together with a present of some Malmsey wine, which prompted Nelson to offer to carry his dispatches to Cádiz for him. Meanwhile, the wounded were being re-embarked and the body of Captain Bowen was buried at sea to the accompaniment of gun salutes and with half-masted colours. The final British casualty list was disproportionately high: 153 killed, drowned or missing and over 100 wounded out of a force of just over 1,000. The comedy of errors had turned into a tragic disaster.

On the afternoon of 27 July, the British squadron finally left the bay of Santa Cruz and headed north for Cádiz. The *Emerald* had already sailed, bearing Nelson's official report. With it, was his first full-length, hand-written letter: a despondent note to Jervis, 'You will excuse my scrawl, considering it is my first attempt' (see illustration on p. 127). Now that the exhilaration of the action was over and the scale of the defeat had begun to sink in, he was in the grips of depression and post-traumatic shock. 'I am become a burthen to my friends and useless to my Country . . . When I leave your command I become dead to the world; I go hence and am no more seen.' That last phrase is an almost exact quotation from Psalm 39, one of the psalms included in the burial service which had just been read over the bodies of the dead. Nelson had obviously been greatly affected by the deaths of so many of his comrades – especially Bowen, 'than whom,' as he wrote in his official report, 'a more enterprising, able and gallant officer does not grace His Majesty's Naval service' (see note on p. 130).

But worse was to come. Among the dangerously wounded was handsome young Lieutenant John Weatherhead of the *Theseus*, who, as we have seen, was one of Nelson's own special protégés. Having landed on the beach close to the mole he was shot in the stomach and was found, close to death, by Bernardo Cólogan who tore up his shirt to make bandages and arranged for him to be returned to his comrades in a special cradle. After lingering, apparently without pain, he finally slipped away on 29 July. 'He was the Darling of the Ship's Company,' grieved his close friend, young William Hoste, '& universally beloved by every person who had the pleasure of his Acquaintance.' Chief among these was Nelson. Lacking sons of his own and disappointed with Josiah Nisbet, he often bestowed paternal affection on particularly promising young officers – and it was one of the tragedies of his life that he often lost them. He wrote to Weatherhead's father:

Believe me, I have largely partaken in our real cause for grief in the loss of a most excellent young man . . . when I reflect on that fatal night, I cannot but

The only portrait of Bowen, taken from his obituary in the Naval Chronicle. *The odd black patch on his right cheek is a flaw in the original engraving.*

Captain Richard Bowen

Richard Bowen's death was regarded as a serious blow by all who knew him. A thirty-six-year-old Devonian from Ilfracombe, he was one of Jervis' most favoured protégés. Having first gone to sea with his father in the merchant service, he transferred to the Royal Navy in 1778 and three years later was Jervis' aide in the *Foudroyant* during her action with the *Pégase*. He was his signal lieutenant in the West Indies and played a key role in the capture of Port Royal in 1794 which won him his promotion first to commander and to post captain a few months later.

He caught up with Jervis again in the Mediterranean in 1796 and was given a number of 'plums', including command of a detached squadron of frigates defending Gibraltar. 'He is a child of my own,' Jervis wrote to the Governor, General O'Hara, 'and you will find in him the most inexhaustible spirit of enterprise and skillful seamanship which can be comprised in any human character.'

Like Miller, whom he resembled in many ways, he was a fine example of the new type of enterprising, and highly professional, young officer with whom Jervis liked to surround himself. Had he lived, he could well have proved a serious rival to Nelson.

bring sorrow and his fall before my eyes. Dear friend, he fought as he had always done, by my side . . . but for wise reasons (we are taught to believe) a separation was to take place.

After a tedious voyage, he finally rejoined the fleet off Cádiz on 16 August. Still in the grips of his black mood, he wrote to his commander, 'A left-handed admiral will never again be considered as useful, therefore the sooner I get to a very humble cottage the better, and make room for a better man to serve the state.' But the new Lord St Vincent (who had just received official notification of his title) would not hear of such an idea. Echoing the message with which he had sent him forth on his mission, he wrote: 'Mortals cannot command success; you and your Companions have certainly deserved it, by the greatest degree of heroism and perseverance that ever was exhibited.'

Rear Admiral Sir Horatio Nelson KB, by Lemuel Abbott. This is the original version of the famous portrait, painted for Nelson's mentor, Captain William Locker. Unlike the better-known, sanitized, copies which Abbott produced later, it gives us a stark and realistic image of Nelson at a time when he was recovering from a horrific and very troublesome wound.

CHAPTER TEN

'A *left-handed admiral*'
Nelson recovers in England

'The moment I am cured I shall offer myself for service.'
Nelson to Lord St Vincent, 9 October 1797

THE JOURNEY HOME

On Sunday 20 August Nelson transferred to HMS *Seahorse* for the voyage home. There he found a very worried Betsey Fremantle, whose husband was still in severe pain from the wound in his arm: 'Admiral Nelson came on board at twelve o'clock,' she recorded in her diary, 'he is quite stout but I find it looks shocking to be without one arm.' There then followed a depressing voyage in a ship full of sick and wounded, 'from morning to night and from night to morning you hear nothing but these unfortunate people groan,' wrote Betsey. In such an environment, and with their own wounds still giving trouble, both her patients became very low-spirited, 'A foul wind,' recorded Betsey on 24 August, 'which makes the Admiral fret, he is a very bad patient, poor Fremantle is the same, no sign of the wounds healing up yet.' And, on 31 August, 'A foul wind again in the afternoon which much annoyed us all. The Admiral is very low and wishes himself back in Cádiz.'

During the voyage, Nelson wrote three letters, each short and painfully executed, their underlying mood of depression confirming Betsey's judgement that he was 'very low'. To his uncle, William Suckling, he wrote asking him to arrange for the Collector of Customs at Portsmouth to take care of his wine and other belongings, 'until I can find a hut to put my mutilated carcase in'. With the pain of his wound, the tedium of the voyage and the ever-present and very audible agony of his fellow sufferers, his black mood had deepened further – the 'very humble cottage' mentioned in his letter to St Vincent, had now become a 'hut'. It was one of the lowest points in his life and he clearly believed that his career was finished.

On 1 September, they finally reached Spithead. Nelson's old patron, Sir Peter Parker was in command at Portsmouth and so he immediately went ashore to Admiralty

House, the splendid official residence in the dockyard, to call on the admiral and his wife. The couple always regarded Nelson 'as a son' and their affectionate welcome, and Margaret Parker's motherly concern, clearly began the cure to his wounded spirit.

But, still more important to his recovery, were the cheers of the crowds. Nelson was detained in Portsmouth for nearly a day and a half, while his formal request 'to go on shore for the recovery of my wounds' was carried up the London road to the Admiralty and the official permission to 'strike your Flag and come on shore' returned and, in that time, he discovered that he was a popular hero. Such a welcome might have been expected in a naval town but, when he arrived in Bath, on 3 September, he found the same adulation awaiting him. The *Bath Journal* reported,

> The Rear Admiral, who was received at Portsmouth with universal greeting, reached Bath on Sunday evening in good health and spirits, to the great joy of his Lady and Venerable father, and the gratification of every admirer of British Valour.

Lady Nelson told Nelson's uncle that 'the Corporation have handsomely congratulated him on his safe arrival' and, within a few days, heart-warming letters began to arrive. 'Such a letter from Lord Hood,' exulted Fanny, 'it does him honour.' The Duke of Clarence wrote to 'congratulate you with all my heart on your safe arrival at last, covered with honour and glory' and Sir Andrew Snape Hammond, the Comptroller of the Navy spoke of his services 'in the most flattering manner'.

This was exactly the medicine that Nelson needed and, under its influence, his natural resilience reasserted itself. 'My general reception from John Bull has been just what I wished' he reported proudly to Lord St Vincent, adding tactfully, 'I assure you they never forget your name in their honest praises.' All thoughts of ending his naval career vanished and, instead, he started looking forward eagerly to returning to sea. Within a month of his return he wrote to St Vincent,

> The moment I am cured I shall offer myself for Service: and if you continue to hold your opinion of me, shall press to return with all the zeal, although not with all the personal ability, I had formerly.

There was, however, one problem: his arm was refusing to heal.

THE TROUBLESOME ARM

On 5 October, Nelson and his wife travelled to Greenwich, to pay a visit to the admiral's old 'sea-daddy', Captain William Locker, now Lieutenant Governor of the Royal Hospital at Greenwich. Nelson was still in so much pain that he had to take opium at night to enable him to sleep and the visit was intended to help his convalescence. But Locker also had another project in mind. Some months before, he had been visited by a Woolwich engraver, Robert Shipster, who wanted to produce a print of Nelson to satisfy the sudden public demand for a likeness of the new hero. Locker had in his collection a splendid portrait of a young, fresh-faced captain by John Rigaud, painted when Nelson had just turned twenty, and Shipster had used this as the basis for an engraving. However, it was difficult for him to know the extent to which Nelson's appearance had been altered by twenty years of hard service and wounds and so it is hardly surprising that the result was rather indifferent. Clearly, something more up to date was required and so Locker approached Lemuel Abbott, who had already painted a number of naval officers.

Abbott came to the hospital for two sittings while Nelson was staying there and produced a rough sketch of him, wearing his undress rear admiral's uniform. The armholes were tight and so the coat sleeve had been slit to enable Fanny, or some other helper, to put a hand inside and ease the heavily bandaged stump into place. At Greenwich, the helper was Locker's young daughter Elizabeth and the bows closing the slit can still be seen in the resulting portrait.

It is, of course, by far the most familiar of all the likenesses of Nelson. Abbott himself made some forty different copies and variants; it was engraved many times and it has been reproduced in almost every biography. But the versions at Greenwich, Portsmouth and the National Portrait Gallery, from which reproductions are most often taken, are all later copies and the further Abbott went from the original, the more he tended to 'adonise' the face. As a result, in the words of leading Nelson portrait expert Richard Walker, Nelson looks like 'a charming sweet-tempered country gentleman not far removed from the breed of Norfolk parsons in which his stock was rooted'. The original sketch and the first version painted for Captain Locker (see p. 132), both still in private hands, show a much starker image of a fighting man – and, moreover, of a man in constant pain. The face is gaunt, the cheeks hollow, the eyes wide and staring and the hair has turned white with shock. The plump-cheeked handsome boy of the Leghorn miniature (see p. 4) and the Cádiz drawing (see p. 113) has become, prematurely, an old man.

Nelson's gaunt appearance in Abbott's original portrait is striking evidence that in early October his arm was still causing a great deal of trouble and worry. Further evidence is to be found in a detailed account of his medical expenses preserved among his personal papers at the Nelson Museum in Monmouth. Using this, it has been possible to reconstruct fully, for really the first time, the convoluted process of consultation and treatment which he had to endure. The total cost was £135 1s 0d – more than two months' pay – but he was eventually able to reclaim the money from the Admiralty (see note on sources p. 147).

In Bath, the wound was dressed by a surgeon, Mr Nicholls, while Mr Spry (presumably a pharmacist) provided medicines – probably laudanum. Nelson also consulted a physician, Dr William Falconer (see illustration on p. 137); but Falconer, who specialized in rheumatology at the Bath Royal Mineral Hospital, was more used to the valetudinarians who came to take the waters at the famous

Sir Horatio Nelson. This engraving by William Barnard, based on Abbott's portrait, shows Nelson standing in front of the burning town of Santa Cruz, and is clearly meant to give the impression that he had succeeded at Tenerife. In fact, the British attack had been bloodily repulsed and little damage done to Spanish property.

Dr William Falconer MD, FRS (1744–1824), from a portrait by Thomas Redmond, after Thomas Lawrence. Falconer treated Nelson when he first arrived in Bath and the two men became friends. Lady Nelson later told her husband that the doctor 'declares had he been a single man he would have embarked with you!'.

spa than the war injuries of military men. He recommended that Nelson should consult an eminent London surgeon, Mr William Cruikshanks, well known for his anatomical studies in association with John Hunter.

So the Nelsons travelled to London, arriving there on 18 September, and took lodgings at 141 Bond Street. But even the eminent Mr Cruikshanks was unable to be of much assistance. There was little doubt about the actual cause of the trouble: one of the ligatures was still fixed in the wound and, as a result, the stump had become infected (see note on p. 138). But there was much less certainty about a cure. At one point, there was even worrying talk of further surgery to release the ligature; since the stump was already very short, this would have been an extremely difficult and painful operation. However, on 12 October, Nelson appeared before the Court of Examiners of the Surgeon's Company at their new premises in Lincoln's Inn Fields (now the Royal College of Surgeons of England). The purpose of the examination was to assess the damage to his right eye, Nelson having had no opportunity to attend earlier for this purpose as he had not previously been in England since receiving the wound. The proceedings were presided over by Sir James Earle, Master of the Surgeon's Company and Surgeon-extraordinary to the King. It would seem that Nelson must have mentioned the problems he was encountering with his arm for, just one week later, Earle examined him again, with the help of two men who both had considerable experience of war wounds, John Rush, Inspector General of Hospitals and later a member of the Army Medical Board, and Thomas Keate who later became Surgeon General to the Army. Their joint, firm advice (which cost Nelson three guineas) was that the cure should be left to time and nature.

In the light of this advice, Nelson decided to dispense with the services of the expensive Mr Cruikshanks and turned, instead, to an old service colleague, Michael Jefferson, who happened to be in London, having just received his official qualification from the Company of Surgeons. He took over the daily dressing of the infected stump and, just over a month later, Nelson woke from an unusually sound and lasting sleep to find that his wound was nearly free from pain. When the hastily summoned Jefferson undid the bandages, the ligature came away with them.

It was a moment for relief and thanksgiving. On 8 December, the Revd Mr Greville, parish priest of St George's Church, Hanover Square received a handwritten note, 'An Officer desires to return Thanks to Almighty God for his perfect recovery from a severe Wound, and also for many mercies bestowed upon him. (For next Sunday)'. And Jefferson, who had previously served with Nelson as a surgeon in Corsica and had signed the certificate relating to his eye wound, now found himself the subject of his patron's habitual warm-hearted gratitude towards anyone who helped him. When the admiral returned to sea the following spring in

---

What was the matter with Nelson's arm?

The common practice with amputations at that time was to tie up the severed arteries with ligatures, with the ends left dangling from the wound. Once the arteries below the ligatures had rotted – usually within a few weeks of the operation – the ligatures were pulled away. Only one of Nelson's ligatures had been freed; the other was still fastened firmly inside the stump.

Because of the excruciating pain he suffered, especially when the ligature was pulled, Nelson thought that, in the darkness of the *Theseus'* cockpit, Eshelby had inadvertently gathered up a nerve in the ligature. He mentioned this theory in a letter to St Vincent on 6 October and it has been often repeated in subsequent accounts, including ones by medical experts (e.g., Pugh, p. 12). However, in a letter to his wife of 5 October, describing the wound (Minto, vol. III, p. 2), Lord Minto recorded an alternative theory (which, presumably, had come from Nelson): namely, that the ligature had been fastened to a *sinew*. This would certainly explain why it remained fixed for so long.

In fact, such speculation is really irrelevant. The main cause of the trouble was in fact the ligature itself rather than what it was attached to. So long as it remained in the wound, its presence caused continuing infection, thus further contributing to Nelson's pain.

HMS *Vanguard*, Jefferson went with him as the flagship's surgeon – a remarkable leap for a comparative junior, and a striking demonstration of the power of patronage in the late eighteenth-century Navy.

THE AMPUTEE ADAPTS

Although his physical recovery was now complete, Nelson still had to adapt to life as an amputee. There were practical adjustments to make, the most obvious of which was the switch to left-handed writing. His early, very wobbly, attempts soon matured into a slightly laborious, upright script, very different to the rapid, sloping scrawl of his right-handed days, and this, in its turn, developed into the more compact, rounded writing of his last years. There were changes to his clothes: the empty sleeve pinned across his chest, so familiar from many portraits; specially shortened right-arm sleeves for his shirts; breeches, stockings and shoes instead of half-boots. His pens were cut differently and, at some point, he even acquired a combined knife and fork to enable him to slice up his food for himself.

Then, too, there was a mental and emotional adjustment to be made. He responded to his mutilation in two key and characteristic ways. His strong religious faith enabled him to see his wound as a fortune of war, even as God's will. In his first, painfully executed letter to Fanny he wrote,

> it was a chance of war, and I have great reason to be thankful, and I know it will add much to your pleasure in finding that Josiah, under God's providence, was principally instrumental in saving my life . . . I beg neither you or my father will think much of this mishap. My mind has long been made up to such an event.

In common with many other amputees, he sometimes experienced the sensation of a 'phantom' arm and once told a friend that the experience had confirmed his belief in the immortality of the soul (see note on p. 140).

As well as his faith, Nelson shared with his father and siblings a robust sense of humour, which was brought into play to deal with the new situation. He gave his stump a nautical nickname and his 'fin', as he called it, became part of his public image. 'I'm Lord Nelson; see, here's my fin!' he shouted one dark night in the Baltic, when a ship he was visiting challenged his boat. His colleagues quickly noticed that the 'fin' tended to twitch when he was angry or agitated, 'The admiral is working his fin' they would say, 'Do not cross his hawse, I advise you.'

He was also prepared to make jokes about the loss of his arm. While he was convalescing, he and his family drew up 'The Petition of Admiral Nelson's Left Hand' in which the hand laments that 'in battle, when my noble Master, God bless him, was hewing down the Dons with the right hand, your petitioner remained unemployed' and goes on to ask for 'an equitable, true and perfect equality to be

Nelson's religious faith

Nelson's religious faith was essentially fatalistic: in common with many of his contemporaries, he believed firmly in predestination. In 1793, he wrote in his private journal,

> When I lay me down to sleep I recommend myself to the care of Almighty God, and when I awake I give myself up to His direction, amidst all the evils that threaten me, I will look up to Him for help, and question not but that He will either avert them or turn them to my advantage, though I know neither the time nor the manner of my death, I am not at all solicitous about it because I am sure that He knows them both, and that He will not fail to support and comfort me. (Warner, p. 82.)

This faith shines through in his fine prayers: 'If it is His good providence to cut short my days upon earth, I bow with the greatest submission,' he wrote in his journal on the road to Portsmouth during his final journey to Trafalgar; and, in the more famous Trafalgar prayer, 'For myself individually I commit my life to Him who made me and may His blessing alight upon my endeavours for serving my Country faithfully.'

He always acknowledged the strength that his faith gave him. For example, in 1801, he wrote to Emma Hamilton:

> I own myself a BELIEVER IN GOD, and if I have any merit in not fearing death, it is because I feel that His power can shelter me when he pleases, and that I must fall whenever it is His good pleasure. (Morrison, vol. II.)

established between us'. These jokes continued throughout his life. When he arrived in Great Yarmouth after his triumphal tour of Europe in November 1800, the patriotic landlady of the Wrestlers' Inn asked permission to rename her pub the Nelson Arms. 'That would be absurd,' came the reply, 'seeing I have but one.' A year later, returning to Great Yarmouth after Copenhagen, he called at the naval hospital to visit men wounded in the battle and, stopping at the bed of a young sailor who had lost his arm, commented 'Well then Jack, you and I are spoiled for fishermen.' And, as he pushed his way through the cheering crowds in Portsmouth, during his last walk on English soil on the morning of 14 September 1805, he was heard to say that he was sorry he did not have two arms, so that he could shake hands with more of his admirers. The evidence suggests, therefore, that Nelson adjusted quickly to his disability and was not unduly concerned by it.

He even used a joke about his arm to cover a royal gaffe. On 25 September, he attended the first 'levee' of the season at St James' Palace. This was a formal reception at which men of the moment were introduced to the monarch – but the notoriously tactless George III had not been well briefed. 'You have lost your right arm!' he exclaimed, when Nelson was presented. 'But not my right hand,' replied Nelson, quickly turning to one of his companions, 'as I have the honour of presenting Captain Berry.' Earlier that day, he had been formally invested by the King with the Order of the Bath: an impressive occasion which must have appealed to his taste for outward show. Two Knights Companion, in their crimson satin robes, brought the new knight before the sovereign and Lord Malmesbury, recently returned after the failure of his latest peace mission, handed the sword of state to the King. Nelson knelt to receive the accolade, the red ribbon he had so coveted was placed over his right shoulder and he then kissed hands and withdrew.

THE HERO

The visit to St James' was but one of a number of public engagements which he undertook at this time – even while he was still in pain from his wound. For Nelson was now revelling in the popular acclaim for which he had worked so hard; as he told Miller, 'John Bull does not forget the *Captain* on the 14th February'. Blame for the failure at Santa Cruz tended to be laid at the door of the politicians, who the press supposed had ordered the attack, and Nelson himself fêted as a hero:

> Protected by such as NELSON, we may defy the malignant threats of our Enemies and look with contempt upon the wild project of an Invasion, confiding in the superintendance of Providence to afford us safeguard, and in our wooden walls.

Similar sentiments were expressed in the City of London on 28 December, when he was presented with the Freedom of the City of London in a gold box by the Chamberlain, John Wilkes. In reply, he made one of his first recorded public speeches, pledging that 'my hand and my head shall ever be exerted, with all my heart, in defence of my King, the Laws and the just liberties of my Country'.

He was also much in demand from artists. One of Abbot's chief rivals, Henry Edridge, produced a formal drawing showing a rather austere and distant figure, leaning elegantly on his sword and looking more like a gentleman of fashion than the untidy, boyishly eager man with the 'shock head' that all his friends described so affectionately. The tumbling hair was captured vividly by the sculptor Lawrence Gahagan, who also managed to catch a trace of Nelson's distinctive 'sweet smile'

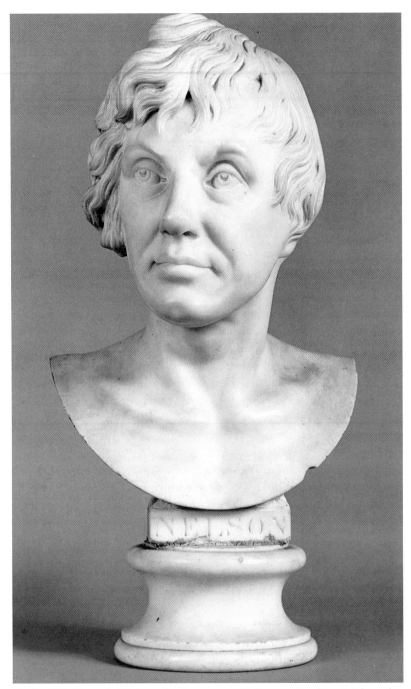

Rear Admiral Sir Horatio Nelson by Lawrence Gahagan. In this vivid, and very realistic sculpture, Gahagan managed to capture both Nelson's 'shock head' and his distinctive smile.

Sir Horatio Nelson by Daniel Orme. Nelson as Byronic hero. This small engraving by Daniel Orme was extremely popular and the first edition sold out in a few days.

that contemporaries also mentioned – at least until the loss of his front teeth in later life forced him to keep his mouth closed (see opposite). But it was Daniel Orme, with his miniaturist's eye, who produced a likeness which best captured Nelson's energy and charisma and satisfied the public demand for an image of The Hero of Cape St Vincent. His engraving, published in February 1798 was an immediate success. 'Orme must have made a great deal of money,' wrote Fanny Nelson to her husband shortly afterwards,

> the little picture he published of you has sold beyond description. Mrs Tarleton as soon as she heard you were to be bought, she was determined to have you, but was told by the bookseller he had had a load of Admiral Nelsons but had sold every one of them.

This was a happy time for Fanny Nelson, perhaps the happiest period in her marriage. After an initial, and understandable, shrinking she learned how to dress her husband's wound and even wrote some of his letters for him until he became more practised with his left hand. Nelson responded to her kindness with his usual infectious enthusiasm; the formidable Lady Spencer, wife of the First Lord of the Admiralty, was charmed into relaxing her usual rule of not noticing officers' wives by an earnest assurance that 'he was convinced I must like her. That she was beautiful, accomplished; but above all, that her angelic tenderness towards him was beyond imagination.' In the vivid reportage of a consummate gossip, we catch another echo of Nelson's direct and eager way of speaking.

The couple behaved at times as if they were newly-weds. Lady Spencer was even persuaded to invite Fanny to a formal dinner at Admiralty House and to place her next to her husband – then, as now, an unusual arrangement for a fashionable table – so that Fanny could cut up his food for him. On a visit to Bath, apparently without Fanny, Nelson found himself in a box at the theatre that contained 'some of the handsomest ladies' in the town; 'but as I am possessed of everything which is valuable in a wife, I have no occasion to think beyond a pretty face'. The valuable wife had also, after so many years of living in rented accommodation, found the cottage which had been so often mentioned in their letters – although 'cottage' was hardly an appropriate word to describe Round Wood. A four-bedroomed house just outside Ipswich, with two 'genteel parlours', a dressing room and wine vaults, it was surrounded by 50 acres of grounds, in which were a barn, dairy, stables, a cow-house and a 'well-planted garden'. Nelson bought the property for £2,000 on 13 November, after the couple had paid a flying visit to inspect it. However, the legal business took some time to conclude and before they could take formal possession he was back at sea.

RETURN TO ACTIVE SERVICE

While Nelson was recovering, the war had entered a new phase. Lord Malmesbury had been able to attend Nelson's investiture at St James' because his second peace mission – 'the late puppet show and burlesque at Lille', as one of the opposition newspapers dubbed it – had ended, like his first, in failure. A *coup d'état* in Paris on 4 September had brought in a more hard-line government, dominated by the military, and the negotiations at Lille were abruptly broken off. Pitt and his ministers had made strenuous efforts to secure peace – they had even offered the French recognition of their control of the Netherlands, thus abandoning the very principle for which Britain had originally gone to war. But now it was clear that France was determined to continue hostilities and so Britain had to set about constructing a new coalition to replace the one shattered by the French victories in 1796.

A few weeks later, morale was raised by another major naval success – this time, against the Dutch in the North Sea. News of Admiral Duncan's victory at Camperdown on 11 October reached London at dawn on the 13th and the capital erupted in relieved celebrations. At one point a rampaging crowd hammered at the door of 141 Bond Street demanding to know why the windows had not been suitably illuminated. When they were told the name of the wounded officer who was trying to sleep upstairs, they went away quietly, 'You will hear no more of us tonight.'

With the immediate threat of invasion finally lifted, the Cabinet could look once again at the situation in the Mediterranean. Britain's removal of her fleet at the end of 1796 had been used by the Austrians to justify their withdrawal from the war; so

The Revd Edmund Nelson. The portrait of Nelson's father used in most biographies gives the impression of a dull and ponderous man. This posthumous likeness captures his gentleness – and the good humour which he passed on to his son.

ministers knew that if they wished to construct a new coalition against France, they had to make a show of strength in the area once again. But with Spain and the Netherlands still allied with France, the problems of supply were as great as ever; so, instead, the idea began to take shape of sending a special detached squadron to operate independently in the Middle Sea. It would be a highly responsible command, for which special qualities of leadership would be required.

Nelson, at this time, was still frustrated at the lack of progress with his arm and longing to get back to sea: 'panting to be in Actuall Service', as his father put it; but, ironically, by holding him in London at this critical moment in the war, his troublesome wound actually worked in his favour. If he had remained with the fleet off Cádiz, his exploits would have soon been forgotten, especially once they were overshadowed by the news of Camperdown. But his regular attendance at Court, and at official Admiralty functions, kept him in the public eye – and, most important, in the minds of influential men such as Lord Spencer – while his empty sleeve was a visible reminder of his extraordinary deeds.

He returned to active service in the spring of 1798, hoisting his flag in HMS *Vanguard* at Spithead on 29 March and eventually setting sail on 10 April. Having rejoined Lord St Vincent off Cádiz on 30 April, he was immediately sent back into the Mediterranean in command of a detached squadron and with the specific task of discovering the destination of a large French expeditionary force known to be assembling in Toulon. When it came to selecting the right man for this responsible command, St Vincent again, as so often in 1796 and 1797, instinctively turned to his most promising junior. And, as before, his trust was not misplaced: for three months later, on 1 August, the ships of Nelson's squadron finally tracked down their French opponents and almost obliterated them at the Battle of the Nile.

When the news of the stunning victory reached Britain, everyone wanted to claim the credit for having selected Nelson. The Duke of Clarence wrote to his friend to assure him that his appointment had been the King's idea. Lord Minto wrote reporting a conversation in which he had suggested the idea to Lord Spencer. Spencer did indeed write to St Vincent, 'If you determine to send a detachment I think it almost unnecessary to suggest to you the propriety of putting it under the command of Sir H. Nelson', but by the time this letter arrived off Cádiz, St Vincent had already detached Nelson on his mission.

So, it seems that everyone had the same idea at once: by the spring of 1798, Nelson's earlier exploits had so singled him out from his fellows that he was seen, quite simply, as the right man for the job. As Spencer put it, his 'acquaintance with that part of the world, as well as his activity and disposition, seem to qualify him in a peculiar manner for that service'.

The Nile certainly made Nelson an international hero, but it was his exploits at Cape St Vincent and Tenerife which positioned him for his great success. Undoubtedly, 1797 was Nelson's year of destiny.

✳ ✳ ✳

SOURCES FOR PART THREE

Previous accounts of the Cádiz and Tenerife operations have been largely based on Nelson's official correspondence as printed in Nicolas and, of course, this material forms the basis of my own narrative, together with the memoirs and diaries of others who were there – for example, William Hoste, William Webley and Betsey Fremantle.

However, in my attempt to produce a more balanced account than has hitherto been available, I have benefited greatly from being the first English writer to have access to all the new Spanish material that has emerged as a result of the bicentenary celebrations and which has been published (mostly in Spanish) in two invaluable books: *Fuentes Documentales del 25 de Julio de 1797*, edited by P. Ontoria Oquillas, L. Cola Benitez and D. Garcia Pulido (containing transcripts of all the key Spanish and British documents) and *La Gesta del 25 de Julio de 1797*, published by Ayuntamiento de Santa Cruz de Tenerife (an illustrated catalogue of exhibits in the special bicentenary exhibition). British readers will find most of this new material superbly distilled into a new account of the battle, seen from the Spanish point of view, by my colleague Agustín Guimerá Ravina, to be published by The 1805 Club in 1999.

I have also been most fortunate to be allowed access to a fascinating – and hitherto unknown – narrative of Cádiz and Tenerife by Ralph Miller. This was discovered recently by Kirstie Buckland among the papers of Sir Thomas Molyneaux, who was acquainted with Miller's sisters. It is a frank and very detailed account, which answers a number of the questions that have hung over both operations for so long – and will soon be available to a wider audience thanks, once again, to the enterprise of The 1805 Club.

The material on the blockade of Cádiz and its effects on the local economy is taken from the article by Agustín Guimerá in the *St Vincent 200* conference papers.

The reconstruction of the convoluted process of consultation and treatment which Nelson endured after the loss of his arm is based on Jessie Dobson's article, 'Lord Nelson and the expenses of his cure', and further material supplied by Leslie LeQuesne and by Jonathan and David Falconer, descendants of Dr William Falconer. Nelson's account for medical expenses and the correspondence relating to it is printed in Naish (pp. 377–9).

The material on the various portraits of Nelson is drawn from *The Nelson Portraits*, by Richard Walker: a masterly work of scholarship published in 1997, which is surely destined to become the definitive work on the subject.

The delightful quotations from the letters of Nelson's father and the 'Petition of Admiral Nelson's Left Hand' come from *The Nelsons of Burnham Thorpe* by E. Eyre Matcham.

The captured enemy colours. Officers from the victorious British fleets escort the captured French, Spanish and Dutch colours in the Grand Royal Procession to St Paul's.

St Paul's Cathedral, London
19 December 1797

At 1000, on Tuesday 19 December 1797, the guns at the Tower of London fired a salute to signal that the royal procession had set out from St James' Palace. King George III, accompanied by Queen Charlotte and their children, was attending a grand service of thanksgiving in St Paul's Cathedral to celebrate 'the many signal and important victories obtained by our Navy in the course of the present war'.

It was a fine, sunny day and the streets were packed with spectators, who crowded into the windows overlooking the processional route and even clambered on to ledges to get a good view. They were treated to what a newspaper called, 'perhaps the finest equestrian spectacle ever seen in any country'. The State Coach, carrying the King and Queen, was drawn by eight cream Hanoverian horses; the Duke of York's by six greys; the Duke of Clarence's by six roans; the Duke of Gloucester's by six bays and the remaining twenty coaches of the Household were pulled by coal black horses.

Following the collapse of the First Coalition and the failure of Lord Malmesbury's peace mission, the government felt that a morale-boosting gesture was required and had decided to highlight Britain's victories at sea. The spectacle was a major national event, attended by the entire Establishment: the royal carriages were preceded by the carriages of the members of the Lords and the Commons, as well as the whole judiciary.

The royal procession reached St Paul's at 1115 and, as the royal party climbed the steps to the great west door, the crowd could see that they had all dressed specially, in honour of the occasion. The King wore a plain dark blue and gold coat and the Queen and Princesses were resplendent in a deep rich blue, similar to the 'mazarine' shade used in Worcester porcelain, with head-dresses of gold and white feathers. The King was greeted at the door by the Bishop of London and the Dean and Chapter of St Paul's and then, as the assembled bands struck up the Grenadiers March, he led his family up the nave, preceded by the Sword of State carried by the First Lord of the Admiralty, Lord Spencer, dressed in his

The Grand Royal Procession to St Paul's, 19 December 1797. In an impressive morale-boosting exercise, King George III and Queen Charlotte go in procession to St Paul's Cathedral to give thanks for the great victories won by the Royal Navy.

crimson parliamentary robes. As the King passed, the packed spectators applauded politely.

The royal procession was supposed to move straight into the choir, where a chair had been placed for the King under a crimson canopy of state. But, when he reached the vast open space under the great dome, his eye was caught by the naval officers assembled there, waiting to play their part in the ceremony and, singling out Admiral Lord Duncan, whose victory at Camperdown two months before was still fresh in the minds of all, he stopped briefly to speak to him. As he turned to continue on his way, the Queen, followed by all the Princesses, swept the officers a deep curtsey.

Once the royal family had taken their places, the service of Holy Communion began with prayers and the Litany. But the usual form was interrupted after the first lesson. The newly appointed cathedral organist, Thomas Attwood, began the elaborate introduction to Henry Purcell's celebratory anthem, 'I will give thanks unto thee oh Lord with my whole heart' and, as the soloists high in the organ loft came in with the first choral section, the naval officers marched in procession through the choir screen.

They brought with them a remarkable collection of captured enemy colours: each flag displayed on a pole, to which was attached a sign indicating the battle at which it had been taken. First came a brace of French tricolours: some captured at the Glorious First of June three years before; others taken in two smaller-scale actions in 1795. Bringing up the rear was Duncan, his supporters carrying Dutch flags captured at Camperdown. But, before them, the stream of red, white and blue was punctuated by the vivid yellow and red flags of Spain, captured at Cape St Vincent. Lord St Vincent was off Cádiz, still watching the Spanish fleet, so these trophies were escorted by Admirals Thompson and Waldegrave – supported by Rear Admiral Sir Horatio Nelson, KB.

As the full choir brought the anthem to its exultant close, the flags were handed to the Dean and Chapter who arranged them on either side of the altar. The escorting officers then returned to their places and the service continued with the singing of the *Te Deum*.

As Nelson handed over the Spanish colours, he stood on the spot where his coffin was later to rest during the first part of his State funeral service, just eight years later. Only twelve months before, he had been flattered when 'See the conquering hero comes' was played in his honour at a provincial ball in Elba. Now he had taken his place on the national stage.

Captain Ralph Miller's Account of the Battle of Cape St Vincent

Captain Ralph Miller wrote this account of Cape St Vincent to his father from the Tagus on 3 March 1797. At some stage, it found its way into the Nelson Collection at Lloyd's. It was not included in Warren Dawson's catalogue of the collection (published in 1932) and, so far as I have been able to ascertain, it has not been used in any previous account of the battle. It was published, with my accompanying notes, in the *Trafalgar Chronicle* (1997). I am grateful to The 1805 Club for permission to reprint it here.

Miller's letter does not offer us any startling new information; rather it throws slightly different light on some of the already well-known events: for example, his vivid description of the *Captain*'s crucial intervention at the crisis of the battle: '. . . turning them as two shepherd's dogs wou'd a flock of sheep'.

The letter is neatly written but, in order to save paper (and thus postage) Miller has crossed his pages twice – once horizontally and then again vertically. It is, therefore, occasionally a little difficult to read. In the transcription below, I have carefully followed his spelling and punctuation (except that, for clarity, ships' names are given in italics). There is one small tear where the seal has been removed, taking a few words with it: where these have been reconstructed, they are shown in [square brackets].

A few notes have been added to highlight and/or explain those passages which are of particular interest.

Captain in the Tagus 3ᵈ March 1797.
I sit down with an heart full of joy to tell my Rever'd and Beloved Father that I have now obtain'd with respect to my profession the grand wish of my heart, the ship I had the honour to command under the Board Pendᵗ of my Gallant

Commodore having been remarkably signaliz'd in the glorious action of the 14th of Feby. in which she was incessantly engag'd from noon till 5 minutes before 4 o'clock; when, as the finish of our days work, after a few minutes action almost brushing sides with the *St. Nicholas* of 80 guns, in which she kill'd and wounded us fifteen or sixteen men; having previously prepar'd for boarding we luff'd our spritsail yard right across her Quarter Deck when the Commodore, at the head of the Boarders enter'd her Quarter Galley from our Cathead[1] and others along the Bowsprit and Spritsail yard to her Quarter Deck, and having driven the Spaniards below and struck her Colours from her boarded the *San Josef* of 112 Guns which immediately surrender'd being foul of the *St. Nicholas* from our having shot away her mizen mast – The Commodore stopp'd me in the act of boarding by an order to remain in the *Captain*, I then caus'd the Spritsail yard to be lash'd to *St. Nicholas*'s Mizen rigging to preserve our Bridge till we had pour'd in Men enough and receiv'd by its means such prisoners as we thought convenient. We had before this, assisted by the Gallant Capt. Troubridge only, attack'd a body of 17 sail of the line running across their hawses till we reach'd the Admiral in the *Santissima Trinida* [*sic*] firing at them in flock when they actually haul'd up on the Larboard Tack as we then were and gave over the attempt of joining their other ships before cut off by a masterly manoeuvre of Sir John Jervis and they never join'd again till the business was over. The *Culloden* and ourselves remain'd a full hour the only ships engag'd with this body,[2] the *Santissima Trinidada* of four and two three deck'd ships being our settled opponents, others here and there firing guns at us and *Culloden* whose hands were equally full, and its scarce credible to tell you their Admiral's fire was so much abated by that of the *Captain* that we had hopes as our ships came up of making her our prize, and I have not a doubt but that we shou'd have succeeded if they had not torn our rigging and sails so totally to pieces that we cou'd not keep up and were most reluctantly oblig'd to give up the lead to the *Blenheim*, who gallantly pass'd between the enemy and us. Our battle was then with different ships, and at 3 o'clock we had the pleasure to see the *St. Isidro* strike to the gallant Captain Collingwood who pass'd on without taking possession with the hope of getting hold of the *Santissima Trinidada*, giving our Friend *St. Nicholas* a smart dressing as he went by[3] – When we luff'd across his stern into close action with her we appear'd on tolerably equal terms, she having lost her Miz T. mast and we our fore with every yard wounded and only one brace and one bowline left. We had in the whole 80 kill'd and wounded, not to mention slight scratches which wou'd swell it to about ten more. Ten of the kill'd and fifteen of the wounded were on the Quarter Deck – one of the former was a little Aid de Camp of mine whom I brought from the *Unité*, Poor Boy! he found an early but a glorious death – One of the latter was my noble Commodore who was struck in the side by the splinter of a block and wou'd have fallen had not my arms support'd him[4] – I was shockingly alarmed at the idea of losing him just as his gallantry had won my esteem and affect[ion] as much as twenty years acquaintance under tamer circumstan[ces]. He is a most noble fellow and I at first fear'd it was one of the vill[ainous] grape shot that were continually singing past our heads – Nothing touch'd me but I found when I endeavour'd to take my half boots off to go to bed at midnight that the outside of my left thigh was stiffen'd and bruis'd which I can ascribe to nothing but the wind of a shot – particularly as the one that kill'd our Major of Marines cou'd have pass'd very few inches from it – As we were unable to renew the action our sails and rigging being all cut to pieces, every mast and yard wounded thru shot through, our Mainmast and every Larboard shroud shot away but one, our Foretopmast and jib boom gone – our wheel shot away and the carriages of five guns disabl'd with numberless hits. The Commodore instead of returning to us hoist'd his broad Pendant in the *Irresistable* [sic] but next morning came on board and put a beautiful ring, a Topaz set round with diamonds on my finger as a token of his esteem[5] and indeed I feel satisfied that our friendship will last as long as ourselves – those four glorious hours became more than years in affection – At five o'clock all firing ceas'd – the smaller body having join'd the rear of the Enemy and making the show of coming down to renew the action, which they still might have done with very superior numbers, and I thought our situation wou'd have tempted them to do so as we lay foul of each other between the Fleets, ours not having been able to form to windward of us[6] – in this situation we had likewise the <u>pleasure</u> to find the *St. Nicholas* on fire in the forehold and at the foot of her Main Mast but our Firemen under the direction of Lt. Spicer whom the Commodore put in command of her in a little time extinguish'd it – it was past 6 before we got clear of each other and by 7 we were in tow of the *Minerva* Frigate and labouring incessantly we put the Main Mast out of present danger, the weather being fine, by midnight – our Officers and men all behaved nobly; fighting their guns with a coolness and regularity that I was delighted to see; perhaps the more so from having paid a particular attention to their obtaining every knowledge at them, by causing six guns to be drill'd every day, and being often present at the drill – Tho' I now know the history of all the action from others I have only imperfectly related to you that which came under my immediate observation – I will only say that among the pleasant things of this glorious day one considerable one is there being no drawback, nobody against whom there is a breath of Censure – every ship was at one part or the other of the day engag'd but situation did not admit of all being equally so;[7] perhaps to the *Culloden*'s and our lot fell what never happen'd to two ships before – not only the sustaining so unique a combat so long but actually turning them as two shepherd's dogs wou'd a flock of sheep – Captain Collingwood's part in the *Excellent* was most officer like and distinguish'd and that of Capt. Frederick in the *Blenheim* very much so, and every ship from the little I saw and all I have learnt appears to have been pressing to get her share of it[8] – On the 11th several of our Frigates from Porto Ferara join'd us, immediately after which the Adm. made signal to prepare for battle and kept frigates far out in all directions between this time and that of the action, this signal was twice and that for keeping close order frequently repeated – the 13th at Noon the *Minerva* with Commodore Nelson on board join'd the Fleet – and in the evening we hoisted his Broad Pendant in this Ship – About ½ past two the morning of the 14th we saw the flashes and heard the reports of many guns to the Southward of us which we knew must be the Spanish Fleet – We were then standing to the S.E. with a fine Breeze at SSW. – This glorious day open'd in Haze, a fine breeze and smooth water, it found our fleet in close order of sailing in two Lines, as the ascending Sun gradually dispell'd the Haze, signals for more and more strange ships were made by the Weather Ships and Frigates, and the signal to prepare for Battle between 8 and 9 – at ½ past 10 thro' the remaining haze we discover'd the Spanish Fleet steering about S.E. and 5 or 6 miles distant from us. We were standing S b W on the Starboard Tack our worst sailers under all plain sail, at 20 mins. past 11 the Admiral made signal to form the Line as convenient and presently after to alter course in succession to SSE, at 40 mins. past 11 DoDo one point to starboard and instantly after to cut thro' the Enemy's Line in which there was an opening – At ¼ before 12 our Van began to engage passing part of the Enemy who had wore on different tacks and cutting thro' the opening in their Line, the *Culloden* who had been in chase leading. At 12 we open'd our fire, at ¾ past[9] the signal was made to come to the wind in succession on the starboard tack – At ½ past 12 signal was made for the Ships that had pass'd thro' to close to each other and tack in succession in which they were follow'd by the Fleet – The *Culloden* however who was far ahead and to windward kept all sail and tack'd, without waiting we a little after at 10 minutes before one wore ship without waiting our turn on the Commodore's observing that immediately the Enemy pass'd our sternmost ship they bore up together with an evident inten[tion] of rejoining those cut off by us; and there being only two of our Ships astern of us we were in a few minutes engag'd again laying in their hawses, as I have before describ'd, the *Culloden* having at the same time if not a few minutes earlier brought their rear to action – the rest of our ships stood on to tack in succession according to the former signal – The Spanish seperated Ships were engag'd by our ships before they tack'd, and when ours did tack, they stood on so far that they fetch'd far to windward of their beaten friends and did not join them till five o'clock as before describ'd – Having come to the end of my Paper / I'm reluctantly My Dear Father oblig'd to take my leave of you requesting you to give my kindest love and duty to My Amiable Mother – tenderest Love to My Dear Patsy and good old Aunt – a thousand kisses to the Little ones and Best respects and best wishes to Mr. and Mrs. Dalrymple and all Friends – Every your most dutiful and affect. Son – R.W. Miller.

Your old Friend Coffin[10] who is as busy as a bee and almost in fuller possession of the Portugese Dockyard then they are themselves desires me to say everything thats friendly for him; he takes a quiet dinner with me tomorrow to talk over old stories and we shall not forget to drink our friends at N. Berwick as we have done many a time at Ajaccio. I do not think he has a much greater favourite in the world than yourself – Tho' we were made a wreck of in the Action, no stick but the Bowsprit being unwounded I hope yet to be ready for sea before several of the Fleet – My Commodore is still in the *Irrestable* [*sic*] but will return to us after his Cruise. Did I tell you in one of my former letters that while Coffin and I were close together working in his garden at Ajaccio a ball pass'd close over our heads that was fir'd at him by a Corsican Rascal he had discharg'd from the Yard? a common amusement in that Island.

Notes

1. The reference to the cathead is an interesting little additional detail. Nelson's account says simply that his party broke through 'the upper quarter-gallery window'.
2. Miller here (as one might expect) repeats Nelson's claim that the *Captain* and *Culloden* fought alone for an hour. As explained in the main text (see p. 78), this claim is not supported by the accounts of those in other ships.
3. This is useful confirmation of the movements of Collingwood's *Excellent* – and, in particular, confirms that Collingwood did not join Nelson at once, as most older accounts of the battle suggest. Instead he arrived about 1½ hours after the *Captain* had become engaged.
4. This is the fullest account that has yet come to light of Nelson's St Vincent wound and Miller gives us some useful new details: the exact nature of the projectile that hit him and, most interesting of all, the fact that the blow was so severe that it knocked Nelson into Miller's arms.
5. The story of the presentation of the ring has been known since 1845, when Sir Nicholas Harris Nicolas was told it by Miller's sister. He included it as a footnote on p. 342 of volume 2 of his *Dispatches and Letters*, where the implication was made (often followed by Nelson's biographers) that the event occurred on the evening of the battle. However, Miller's own account makes it clear that the presentation was made the day after the battle and that Nelson paid a special visit to the *Captain* to effect it – a characteristic gesture.
6. This statement clashes with other accounts, including Drinkwater's, whose plans show the British line to *windward* of the *Captain* at the end of the battle and protecting her from the Spanish.
7. Here Miller confirms what all the other accounts say: '. . . There being no drawback, nobody against whom there is a breath of censure.' Collingwood had used almost exactly the same words in a letter to his uncle on 22 February.
8. At this point Miller, realizing he still has a whole page left, goes back to the beginning of the battle and fills in some extra details.
9. This is a mistake on Miller's part: he presumably means quarter past (Jervis' first signal to tack was in fact made at 1208, *Victory*'s time, which was a little behind the *Captain*'s time).
10. Sir Isaac Coffin was a contemporary of Nelson's having been born in May 1759 and entered the Navy in May 1773. He saw much distinguished service in the War of American Independence but then ruptured himself badly while rescuing a drowning sailor. Thereafter, his service was entirely ashore as Commissioner successively of the dockyards at Corsica, Lisbon, Minorca, Halifax, Sheerness and Portsmouth. For these notable services, he was created a baronet in 1804.

Nelson's letter to General Gutiérrez

The version of Nelson's letter to Gutiérrez printed in Nicolas (vol. II, p. 421) was copied from a transcription in James Harrison's 1806 biography, which had been much 'improved' and so was very inaccurate. I am grateful to my colleague Agustín Guimerá Ravina, who arranged for me to see and transcribe the original letter, which is now preserved in the Museo del Ejercito de Madrid.

The body of the letter is in a clerk's handwriting – but the signature is in Nelson's left hand. It is extremely shaky and is strongly suggestive of a man suffering great pain and shock.

Theseus off Teneriffe 26 July 1796 [*sic*]

I cannot quit this Island without returning Your Excellency my sincerest thanks for your kind attention to myself and your humanity to those of our wounded who were in your possession or under your care as well as your generosity to all that were landed which I shall not fail to represent to my Sovereign and I hope at some future period I may have the honor of personally assuring Your Excellency how much I am Your Excellencys Obedient Humble Servant.
Horatio Nelson

I beg Your Excellency will honor with your acceptance a Cask of English Beer and a Cheese

Don Antonio Gutiérrez
Comd Genl de las Islas de Canaria

Bibliography

The Annual Register, 1797

Anson, W.V., *The Life of John Jervis, Lord St Vincent*, London, 1912

Ayuntamiento de Santa Cruz de Tenerife, *La Gesta del 25 de Julio de 1797*, Tenerife, 1997

The *Bath Journal*

Bosanquet, H.T.A. 'Lord Nelson and the loss of his arm', *Mariner's Mirror* 38

Brenton, E.P. *Life of Lord St Vincent*, 2 vols, London, 1838

Buckland, K., *The Miller Papers*, The 1805 Club, 1999

Clarke, J.S. and M'Arthur, J. *The Life of Admiral Lord Nelson*, 2 vols, London, 1809

Churchill, T.O. *The Life of Lord Viscount Nelson*, London, 1808

Collingwood, Newnham. *Correspondence and Memoirs of Lord Collingwood*, London, 1828

Corbett, J.S. (ed.). *The Spencer Papers*, 4 vols, NRS, 1913–24

Dobson, Jessie. 'Lord Nelson and the expenses of his cure', *Annals of the Royal College of Surgeons of England*, vol. 21, 1957

Drinkwater, John. *Narrative of the Proceedings of the British Fleet commanded by Admiral Sir John Jervis, KB, in the late action with the Spanish Fleet*, London, 1797; 2nd, expanded, edition, London, 1840

Fenwick, K. *HMS Victory*, London, 1959

Fremantle, A. *The Wynne Diaries*, London, 1937

Fremantle, S. 'Nelson's first writing with his left hand', *Mariner's Mirror* 35

Gardiner, R. *Fleet Battle and Blockade*, London, 1996

Guimerá, A. *Nelson at Tenerife*, The 1805 Club, 1999

——. 'Commerce and Shipping to Spain during the Napoleonic Wars', *St Vincent 200*, 1998

Harrison, J. *The Life of Horatio Lord Nelson*, London, 1806

Hills, A-M. 'His Belly off Cape St Vincent', *St Vincent 200*, 1998

Hoste, Lady Harriet. *Memoirs and Letters of Captain Sir William Hoste*, 2 vols, London, 1833

Howarth, D. and S. *The Immortal Memory*, London, 1988

Hughes, Edward, (ed.). *The Private Correspondence of Admiral Lord Collingwood*, NRS, 1957

Jackson, J. Sturges. *Logs of the Great Sea Fights*, 2 vols, NRS, 1899–1900

——. 'The tactics of Sir John Jervis', *Naval Miscellany Vol. III*, NRS, 1922

Lloyd, C. *St Vincent and Camperdown*, London, 1967

The *London Gazette*, 1797

Mahan, A.T. *The Influence of Sea Power upon the French Revolution and Empire*, London, 1893

——. *Nelson: The Embodiment of the Seapower of Great Britain*, 2 vols, London, 1897

Matcham, M. Eyre. *The Nelsons of Burnham Thorpe*, London, 1910

Minto, Countess of. *Life and Letters of Sir Gilbert Elliot*, London, 1874

Moriconi E. and Wilkinson, C. 'Sir John Jervis: The man for the occasion', *St Vincent 200*, 1998

Morrison, A. *The Hamilton and Nelson papers* (private collection), 1893/4

Naish, G. *Nelson's letters to his wife*, NRS, 1958

The *Naval Chronicle*

Nicolas, Nicholas Harris. *The Dispatches and Letters of Lord Nelson*, 7 vols, London, 1844–6

O'Donnell, H. and Gonzalez-Aller, J.I. 'The Spanish Navy in the 18th Century, *St Vincent 200*, 1998

Oman, C. *Nelson*, London, 1947

Oquillas, P.O. and others. *Fuentes Documentales del 25 de Julio de 1797*, Tenerife, 1997

Pack, A.J. *The Man who burned the White House*, Emsworth, 1987

Palmer, M.A.J. 'Sir John's Victory: The Battle of Cape St Vincent Reconsidered', *Mariner's Mirror 77*, 1991

Parsons, G.S. *Nelsonian Reminiscences*, London, 1905

Pocock, T. *Horatio Nelson*, London, 1987

Power, D'Arcy. 'The operation on Nelson in 1797', *British Journal of Surgery*, vol. 19, 1932

Pugh, P.D. Gordon. *Nelson and his surgeons*, London, 1968

Ross, J. *Memoirs and Correspondence of Admiral Lord de Saumarez*, 2 vols, London, 1838

Spinney, J.D. 'Nelson at Santa Cruz', *Mariner's Mirror 61*

Taylor, A.H. 'The Battle of Cape St Vincent', *Mariner's Mirror 40*, 1954

——. 'The Battle of Cape St Vincent', *Naval Review 42*, 1954

The Times

Tucker, J.S. *Memoirs of Admiral the Right Honourable the Earl of St Vincent*, 2 vols, London, 1844

Tulard, J. and others. *Français et Anglais en Méditerranée 1789–1830*, Toulon, 1992

Walker, R. *The Nelson Portraits*, Portsmouth, 1998

Warner, O. *The Life and letters of Vice Admiral Lord Collingwood*, London, 1968

——. *A Portrait of Lord Nelson*, London, 1958

White, C. *The Battle of Cape St Vincent*, The 1805 Club, 1997

——. 'The Battle of Cape St Vincent', *St Vincent 200*, 1998

——. 'Reconstructing the British Line of Battle at Cape St Vincent', *Nelson Dispatch*, 1997

——. 'An eyewitness account of the Battle of Cape St Vincent', *Trafalgar Chronicle*, 1997

Notes

St Vincent 200: 'The Proceedings of the Bicentennnial International Naval Conference, Portsmouth 15 February 1997' (published 1998 by The 1805 Club, in association with the Society for Nautical Research and The Nelson Society).

The *Trafalgar Chronicle* and the *Nelson Dispatch* are the journals respectively of The 1805 Club and The Nelson Society. For details of both these societies, and the addresses of their current secretaries, write to: The Deputy Director, Royal Naval Museum, HM Naval Base, Portsmouth, PO1 3NU.

Index

Page numbers in italics refer to illustrations.

THE THEATRE
OF OPERATIONS
1796-1797

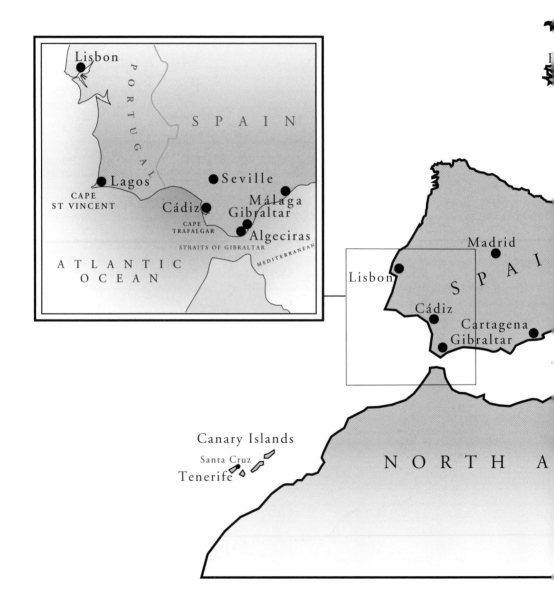

BANTRY BAY

Lisbon

P O R T U G A L

S P A I N

Lagos

CAPE
ST VINCENT

Cádiz

Seville

Málaga
Gibraltar

CAPE
TRAFALGAR

Algeciras

STRAITS OF GIBRALTAR

MEDITERRANEAN

ATLANTIC
OCEAN

Madrid

Lisbon

S P A I

Cádiz

S

Cartagena
Gibraltar

N O R T H   A

Canary Islands

Santa Cruz
Tenerife